What readers say about

"The clearest message for me is: We
suggests gentle, effective ways to make small changes in our daily
lives and help secure a bright future for humanity and for the Earth
that hosts us."   DEB HOY, Editor *Touch* Magazine. UK
(available from www.reikiassociation.org.uk)

"Although this book is an extremely 'easy read', it is one I felt
needed to be taken slowly and steadily to be able to fully digest all
the fascinating and encouraging information within its pages. With
each chapter being devoted to a particular subject, this book answers
many questions whilst opening up new perspectives for the reader
to explore. One of the best channelled works I have seen – it has
certainly given me much on which to ponder."

JOAN OSBOURNE, *Paradigm Shift* Magazine March 2013

"Your book has literally changed my life – it made so much sense to
me and answered so many questions I already had.[...]Thank you so
much – it was transformational."   K. GEORGE

"The message in this book really resonated with me – it has helped
open up a completely new way of thinking about the world we live
in for me. Being a Reiki student, the messages about Reiki were
particularly important for me – especially the benefits of having
Reiki circles infused with joy."   MAMTA NANDA, Reiki Master

"This clearly written, cleanly channelled book is a must for anyone
willing to look at the bigger picture of Earth's history and humanity's
part in her destiny."   KRISTIN BONNEY, Reiki Master

"Amazing account of Atlantis - as real as being there in flesh & blood! I love this book! It made me feel so at home. I was always drawn to Atlantis but could never find enough reliable information that would help me to connect to that past. This book presents Atlantis as if you are physically there and going through its history day by day. This account if alive as well as informative to the last detail. Absolutely amazing! Once I opened the book I literally could not put it down and practically inhaled it. I could read it over and over again and it still feels fresh as if I've never read it before. I can't quite explain it and to be honest don't really want to. I just love it!"

M. BAYLES

"I was very inspired by this book! There was so much hype around 2012. This book gives great insight into the new cycle that was started at that time and prepares us for the changes that may come in so many aspects of our lives. Having read it many months ago, I am surprised at how much there is still to learn from it. Not only is it worth reading, it is worth re-reading."   K. TLUSTY-RISSMAN

"I've loved all of Candace's books; I've read each of them from start to finish with nothing more than a break for meals! Having tried on all religions for size only to find they don't sit well with me, I continued my search for truth, this is the closest I've come to it. It's a book I'll pick up when I need to feel inspired, and when I'm feeling less than charitable towards fellow human beings. It's a great read (all her books are) for anyone struggling to find compassion for others."   KAREN S.

After We Die

Forgotten Truths from Azreal, the Archangel of Death

By Candace Caddick

To Heather,
Enjoy your journey!
Candace

Brightstone Publishing

First published 2019

Published by Brightstone Publishing
7 Blackstone Hill
Redhill, Surrey RH1 6BE
United Kingdom

ISBN registered to me, the author, under Brightstone Publishing.

British Library Cataloguing in Publication Data
A catalogue record for this book is available from the British Library

ISBN 978-0-9565009-5-3

Cover illustration Saharan sunset, courtesy NASA

Dedicated to the memory of Phyllis Lei Furumoto

In appreciation of all the support I received from her in my writing and Reiki practice. I miss her loving presence in my life.

Books by Candace Caddick

Planet Earth Today: How the Earth and Humanity Developed Together and Where We're Going Next (2010)

The Downfall of Atlantis: A History of the Tragic Events Leading to Catastrophe (2011)

And I Saw a New Earth: 2012 and Beyond (2012)

Guidebook to the Future: The Future After 2012 (2013)

Stepping Through the Looking Glass: Life on the Other Side (2016)

After We Die: Forgtten Truths from Azreal, the Archangel of Death (2019)

Acknowledgements

I would like to thank my daughters Pippa and Heather Caddick for their unstinting support for me while writing this book. I'm also grateful for the encouragement of my friends Alison Hopkins, Brenda Hyndman, Marlys Bridge and Grainne Warner. Authors need people asking when the next book will be finished!

Contents

Foreword

The focus of my work when I see private clients is to allow someone's spirit guides to speak to them and give them guidance, to help them on their way. I do not usually bring messages through from their deceased loved ones. Occasionally, on request, we get a message from a family member. Recently I brought through a message of love, where the words were "I love you and our daughter more now than when I was alive with you. I carry the greater love of the universe along with my own love." Words to you, but to me as the bridge between these two people I was awash with the universal love of his present existence. We live on scraps of love on this planet. In death there is so much love available to us, freely given. I am left in admiration of the courage of those who incarnate again and again on a planet where we are so cut off from love.

Introduction

In our previous books we angels have often written about the Earth, a glorious planet that we cherish and protect. She existed before humanity ever set foot on her surface or swam in her seas, and we have had a long relationship with her. She is a sentient planet that develops her own pathways for growth and accepted you as a partner in an adventure in living. After eons, you are nearing the end of your time together in your present forms. Earth is changing rapidly and humanity has to make difficult decisions about how they will finish their game on her surface.

This is a book about death, the release of the physical body and the continuance of the soul's journey on the other side. It includes new information about changes taking place to help humanity. Death can be used like a tool to fine tune the human experience on Earth, by adjusting who is present based on their contributions to the human soul's ascension prospects. This is often based today on how an individual protects other people and the Earth, as caring for others as much as they care for themselves is the final step that everything needed to ascend has been learned. The vast majority of the lessons have now been learned by enough people to carry the soul group over the finishing line into an ascended state. Repairing the Earth shows that the lessons of respect and oneness with others, including your planet, has been learned. At the end, the light in the human soul will be set free to grow in wisdom and joy by taking the next step in your evolution.

Humanity has chosen to enforce it's original plan for dying, a life was over when it had accomplished what it came to Earth to do, and not when old age had been reached. The relationship of the individual soul to the Earth and its efforts on behalf of others will become paramount in determining a person's lifespan. Many people on Earth today have completed their lives and some are living on in pain through fear of dying. This is rarely anyone's chosen way to leave the planet.

Death is a dynamic and active state of being. In death one is fully conscious and it is possible to see clearly what you wish to accomplish next on Earth. It is difficult to have this clarity when in a body once more. This is the purpose in living for every individual, to learn about life to the point where they never need to repeat a lesson again. In the end they will realise that to hurt another is to hurt themselves, whether it is a person, insect or the planet. All life is one.

Archangel Azrael

I have written five previous books with the Archangels and they always want to write about something new, without repetition. Therefore, in the text I have put the names of the previous books near subjects that are explained in greater depth elsewhere, to assist any reader interested in further reading. A little background information is included in the beginning of Part One for those who are new to these books. In this book wherever I have referred to the Creator as He, it is solely to avoid the awkwardness of He/She.

Candace Caddick

Part One
Opening the Gate

1

Clocks are Ticking

B EFORE the beginnings of Western culture, before the Greeks and Egyptians began to influence beliefs about living and dying, there was a greater knowledge of death and the afterlife. Humans and animals lived and died without illness and the degenerative diseases of today. People observed the seasonal growth and death of plants and animals and their own deaths arrived with an acceptance that has long been lost. When a body was old and weary it could be laid aside with the knowledge that death was never the end. Life would always be renewed and loved ones were never lost forever.

What we are describing is flow, from life to death to life again without a hitch or a snag. People were born and died according to a plan made earlier while still in spirit and before they took their first breath as a newborn baby. By conceiving a plan and putting it into action they were able to lay down their bodies and complete their plan regardless of their age. This was not something to be feared or pushed away. Everyone had a chance to say farewell to their families and were able to die peacefully in their presence. When this was the case in every home and family, then death was never feared. The person who had completed this life was free to go "Home", rejoining the greater human consciousness until he or she was ready to venture back for another life on Earth.

Home is where all of you have spent a lot of time, where you can remember who you truly are when not playing a role on Earth, where you use only a tiny part of your own greatness and long experience. When you are Home you are never lonely or bored; you are a splinter of a great universal soul that incarnates on planets on a journey of self-discovery, and to learn about the Creator who made them. The people who can't remember their life plan when they are born, in many cases, will still manage to complete enough of it to learn something new before they die. This way of learning has served humanity well, as a way to grow and deepen as a soul. There would have to be a good reason to change it now.

You need to become aware of a few basic changes that have taken place since 2012 affecting the human soul. One is that the Earth has changed and is swiftly heading towards light herself, taking with her the souls of the many species who live on her surface. She needs everyone to keep up with her own advance towards the light by spending enough time in her company outdoors. This is easy for every life form except humanity living in their cities. Humanity is one of the souls attempting to go with her, but who have built up problems during their stay here by despoiling the Earth for selfish reasons. Of course, some people bear greater responsibility for this than others.

When the human soul first made a contract with planet Earth for a game on her surface they devised a set of rules they intended to live by. We angels felt this was the most astonishingly extreme game that had ever been conceived! The following is from our book *Planet Earth Today* and sets out humanity's original plan to reach ascension. There were many new and unusual aspects to this game.

1.   There was no connection to each other, to any other form of life on the planet or the planet itself, or to the local star.

2.   The higher dimensions were hidden by a thick veil.

3.   The ability to see all the angels of light and dark, the elementals (dryads, dragons, fairies, etc.) and beings of the other dimensions was removed.

4.   The players had no previous memory of all that had been learned across the long eons of this universe and were starting this game as blank and clean as an empty sheet of paper.

5.   The players were prepared to play and play and play with hearts breaking with loneliness. (This was the most extraordinary of the aspects to those of us who watched.)

6.   God was wiped as a memory for them; they wanted to see if they could find him from a position of complete unknowing.

This contract has been altered many times by humanity since its beginnings here; it has been superficially tinkered with. For example, there was the introduction of karma and later the withdrawal of karma. In earlier times you were able to see all the elementals, until they hid themselves from you (as explained in *The Downfall of Atlantis*). These are not breaches of the contract. As your time on Earth nears its end, the heavy veils that hid the higher dimensions from you are being lifted. Some of you today not only see the elementals again as once you were able to, a few are seeing angels and demons, the past and the future, the consistency and texture of energy, etc. These are signs of the maturation of your species as you approach the wisdom of other beings. Animals, for instance, learned quickly what it was to work with the Earth. Those people who can see further than others are at the leading edge of human development, moving forward and at the same time showing the way to those who are following behind. Look around and follow those you feel you can trust as you walk into your future.

However, the greater human soul itself is not required to sit by, watch and do nothing. On the contrary, humanity, in its highest form as a collective of souls, has decided to scrap anything holding it back. What it has decided to do is summon home those whose actions do more harm than good to their fellow humans and the Earth. This irresistible summons is for all those whose time is up and cannot be denied.

This has never happened before with humanity. There was never any need to call back part of the population on the planet. If you feel the Earth is over-populated you could be right in one way, and wrong in another. There is always something to be learned from an extreme situation like over-population. Environmental stresses provide an opportunity for everyone to work together to solve problems. There are people who have dedicated their lives to this, as well as those who only see the profits that can be made from stripping Earth of its resources. Many people never think about it at all, trusting that a scientist somewhere will make sure it turns out alright.

Humanity has run out of time to see if people will join together in saving the planet or destroy it before leaving to colonise elsewhere. Your present timetable here was set long ago, and in 2012 many people, as much as forty-five percent of the Earth's population, made a choice to stay with the reborn Earth for her next life cycle and help care for her. She started a new journey around the galaxy, the final journey in her current form. On her surface were those who chose to stay with her, along with some who never noticed that a choice was being offered. Many of those who chose to stay live away from cities, some by farming around the world. Originally it was assumed that one hundred percent of the human population would be aware of the choice and choose to stay with the Earth.

Today you have a mixture of people on Earth. Those who turned their backs and have been living on a planet Earth whose increasing vibration is unsuited to them, like breathing poison gas. The planet they lived on is long gone. They look to live by all their old values of self-enrichment on a planet that does not support them and without her energy they will die. These people are the ones who are wearing timers on their body clocks showing how close they are to the end of their lives. Many are very near the end now.

When the greater human soul's summons went out to bring home the individuals harming the planet and other life here, it was received by their higher selves who then set about complying with the request. They did not all immediately stop living and leave, but they set their timers to go off and bring forward their life's end for an earlier exit. The timers are ticking for all ages across the decades of life and not just the elderly. These are not seen as a punishment for anyone, but are more along the lines of a coach directing his sports team; humanity is managing its players in order to win the game. The people who are leaving are human, splinters of the same greater soul. They are a part of you, please don't despise them.

This isn't the first time humanity has altered the base rules of its existence here on Earth. A very long time ago you lived below the waves of the oceans, a very good place to learn about the way energy flows. Water flowing in the oceans is one of the greatest sources of light energy on your planet. It was a nursery for you here and when you had experienced flow you stopped and changed, starting again on dry land. You were now able to recognise light and flow whenever you came across it. Everyone learns on Earth through experiencing life.

After 2012, when humanity decided to change the rules for living on Earth, the first one it discarded was the rule of karma. Karma is a very slow way of learning, but it was perfect for the ages it was in use. Slow was necessary and karma was thorough and safe. You could never cut a corner when living with karma and you learned about the universe through cause and effect. It didn't matter that not many were aware they were living daily with karma, it worked anyway. It gave structure and rules to your experience on this planet.

Today you are living in a post-karmic world. It is gone as an energetic force, lingering in the belief systems of those people who haven't noticed it's been absent since 2012. You are in need of speed to keep up with a planet that is racing ahead. Many of those being called home are those who are not ready to learn without the rules of karma. They are the slower learners, they have lived their lives causing more harm than good and would require many karmic lives to learn from the lessons this is creating. Instead, their individual soul will dissolve and be reabsorbed into the greater human soul group and continue to learn through other people's lives and experiences. This is not punishment, but the overarching human soul is nearly out of time on Earth to accommodate the slow learning these people require right now. There are far, far more people who do good, rather than harm, and they are not being called home, or kept back from the planet. There is work for them to do on Earth.

2

Fear of Dying

DURING their long stay on planet Earth humans were born, lived, and died in a circle of life that was free flowing, without snags or hitches to slow down life's easy flow and rhythm. This flow only began to alter a couple of thousand years ago at a time when more people began to live away from the Earth by moving into cities. They missed out on experiencing the seasonal planting cycles of life and death and the births and deaths of animals. Their loved ones died and were taken away to be buried, where before death had been handled by the families. Their mourning was deeply felt but they did not fear what might be happening to their family members after death, and did not believe they were suffering in an afterlife. They still remembered they had an immortal soul that was not lost in death, but was part of their common humanity. Other people were fellow splinters of the same soul, life went on and death was always present without fear.

In the beginning, the human soul considered how long each life would be on Earth, and how it would end. It chose lives of around one thousand years in length (short in our opinion!) to learn about themselves. At the end of that time they would feel their life force diminish and fade. They gathered their families together and lying on their beds they were able to die in peace surrounded by their loved ones, bidding them farewell. Illness did not play a role in bringing lives to an end, only the absence of energy to keep going with vigour. They spent many years living in strength and health until that time. Illness happened so rarely they had little experience of it, although there could be an accident resulting in an early death.

Times changed and the light coming to Earth from the universe had to arrive through clouds of fear and lies. This made a material difference to those living here. They were no longer well-supported by the univrse and disease began to creep in while life spans shortened. We reintroduced healing with the vibration of love in an early form of Reiki healing. The higher vibration of our healing system was the opposite of disease and those who practiced it maintained their health until death. But death came earlier and earlier in spite of this practice of self-healing. There was insufficient light to be found on the dimmed planet as light from the universe was partially blocked by clouds of fear. We angels were busy with our advice and guidance. We did not worry, as worry is not an aspect of light and all experiences of light or dark are valuable to the Creator.

The Earth is able to shine out the light native to her soul into the universe, although not as bright as a star. She shines the light of love and truth, although her light was dimmed under this layer of fear. If you picture a light bulb covered in mud, it's hard to see the light coming through. The dimness on Earth eventually created an environment where people and animals lived in a dense fog and wandered blindly through their lives. It was a very sad situation, still continuing today in many places. The layer of fear is made up of thoughts and beliefs, the greatest being the fear of dying and going into the unknown.

City dwellers became afraid to die, fearful of what came next. In Atlantis the wealthy used cloning to postpone their deaths, driven by their love of money and possessions. In the modern age, fear of what happens after death began to slow the circle of life as people began to hang onto their lives subconsciously once they were near the end.

Visualize this circle of life flowing smoothly today at a steady speed until it bulges and slows with the lives of those who have lived beyond their natural time to die. The bulge acts like a log-jam in a river, only permitting a trickle of water to pass through. This is the way death has slowed down for humanity. People are born knowing on the inside approximately how long they will live, it is written in their genetic code and in their life plans. Now when someone is ready to die they have to push through the thickened energy of the bulge. Some people began to die from painful and unpleasant diseases in hospital as the only sure way they knew to leave the planet. Stagnant energy slowed the process of death at the end of their days. That was the situation until early 2018 when energy was directed to dissolve the log-jam, restoring light and flow.

Our object, as angels and beings of light, is to always foster free flowing energy. We view stagnation and obstructing the flow as darkness. We look always to increase the level of light present on Earth because that is our role in the universe. We bring light, nurture light, plant seeds of light, fight battles with dark angels to keep the light alive and build shields to help keep the darkness at bay. We know that fear is one of the most effective ways to increase darkness, as a dark seed planted and grown by the angels of darkness, i.e. demons. From fear springs many forms of hatred. Lies are another seed frequently used by the dark side. (In our book *Planet Earth Today* the section written by the Archangel of Darkness explains how he uses lies to trick people into following darkness.)

We watched as fear of death and the afterlife increased and spread. New versions of the afterlife began to be made up when that which everyone once knew was forgotten. Very few of them contained any truth at all. They began to introduce fearfulness over the way eternity would be spent after death, usually by being punished. In reality, dying can be as simple as walking from one room into another, just by stepping through a doorway. Some time later you would step back through another doorway and into a new life. There was no resistance, no pain. Nowadays people are often blocking the doorway at the end of their lives with arms and legs braced against the opening, terrified to go through. This saddens us. Other people are weary and trying to leave but can find making their way through the stagnant energy blocking the door very difficult. Some will commit suicide as a quick way to bring their life to an end and bypass the log-jam when it is their time to leave. We did not devise this way of living and dying on Earth, it was conceived by the greater human soul as a way to learn about who they are. Flowing from life to death once worked very well.

Humanity had a single objective in mind when they arranged to come and settle on Earth. They would live here until they remembered that they were a tiny part of the Creator. This would not be the first time they incarnated in physical form and played a long game on a planet, always with the same objective - to remember who they are and where they came from. Every person tries to remember that they were created and provided with life by God. In each previous adventure on different planets humans had accomplished this, absorbing the knowledge into the soul group until it became part of humanity. Every time they devised a new way of experiencing life and death humanity grew with wisdom. One day at the end of the universe, when the Creator begins the long in-breath to draw all of his creation back to him, you will rejoin him and he will learn about himself through your experiences on Earth.

3

Humanity, A Great Universal Soul

AT THE BEGINNING of this universe the Creator set in motion a long game of polarity. Light and dark angels were created to marshal their forces and lead two opposing teams. Angels are a part of God, each created by and beloved by Him. He also created those souls who would learn through incarnating on planets (and stars!) and they devised their own methods of learning in physical bodies. When they fully realised that they were simply a tiny beloved part of God, they were ready to move on and see if they could learn it all over again in a new way. Sometimes they chose not to move on and sealed their planets off behind shields of light to wait until the end of the universe.

The souls that incarnate on planets, like the human soul, learn by doing. The souls that never incarnate on planets (although there are exceptions to every rule) learn by watching and guiding. They can see the bigger picture and are able to guide anyone who is able to hear their voice. Angels learn about planetary games in a second-hand way. We wish to emphasize that planetary games are not the only games in the universe. We also take action all the time, but in a very different way. Angels have our own ways of learning about ourselves and the Creator but we do not experience our existence as you do. We don't have a physical body and so never die and we never forget anything we've learned. We learn one way, you another.

Humanity has never chosen the option to sit still and stagnate. We will say this about you: you are up for absolutely anything! You have used your time in the universe to grow in skill and love and light. You are one of the most creative souls in existence. We can give you an idea in your dreams and you can hand it back improved beyond recognition. Over and over this happens in music, writing and art. We are honoured to work with you, a vast and magnificent soul of light.

Creativity is what you are best at, and when the time comes for everyone to return to the Creator, He will learn how in His vastness he can also create in small ways. One who creates universes can also create a trill on the end of a musical phrase, or a take a narrative and turn it into a story that touches the hearts and imaginations of millions (such as J.R.R. Tolkien.) People live with a spark of God in their hearts and use their lives to demonstrate how they are also able to create. When the Creator receives the information back from all the life He has created He will know more about who He is. Humanity's role is to remember its' connection to Him and remember the love in which you are held.

As a soul of light you have lived on this planet and struggled by not recognising yourself in others. Because you do not see that you are parts of a whole soul you are willing to hurt others, even though you are hurting yourself when you do so. Depriving another human of life is the same as if you cut off one of your hands, never realising it was yours, and feeling all the pain. You do not cherish the diversity and individuality of everyone you meet, but scorn those who differ from you, not recognising your oneness. Treating others the way you wish to be treated yourself is the golden rule to help you grow towards self-knowledge and realise that you are all the same as these diverse and wonderful people. Knowing that you are one with every other person is only the first step towards humanity's ascension from this planet.

When humanity began to devise a new game and create a new learning experience, they looked to partner with a strong planet of light. They wanted the best they could find and the Earth agreed to host them in a risky game. The stakes were huge, if humanity could successfully pull off their new game plan they would take the entire universe with them on a giant leap forward. In this game they would try to remember they were part of God from a complete blankness of unknowing, they would only see three of the twelve dimensions (the twelfth being Divine,) they would not pool the knowledge they learned while alive, contrary to most animal species, neither would they pool their knowledge during the rest times between lives. That last was unheard of in this universe!

The usual way of learning in the universe is that a soul begins a learning experience on a planet by splintering into individual players. These can work very closely together by sharing a hive mind, on Earth the closest you come to this is bees, flocks of birds and schools of fish. They share a lot of common thoughts and experiences and that has been designed as part of their game. A bird who learns something new can pass it on quickly to other living birds until they are all doing the new action across their range. A well known example was when the magpies realised that if they pecked through the shiny top of doorstep milk bottles they could drink the milk. This quickly spread until it was practiced all over Europe.

On Earth when an animal dies and goes back to its soul group, everything it learned while alive is shared with the others who are waiting for their next life. (Most beings rest a little while after they die.) This is an efficient way for a soul to learn. Never assume you know what an animal species is here to learn! Only humanity chose to live and die and never share after death what they learned while alive, but keep it within their own individual consciousness. It is one of the reasons your game on Earth has taken so long. You can only learn from your own mistakes and slowly piece together why you are here using the experiences of your many lifetimes.

Humanity devised this way of learning as an experiment, to see if it were possible to ascend in this manner. The universe is full of experiments, variations upon variations of lives and experiences. All humanity needed was a willing planet to be the host. Arrangements were made and the price agreed: humanity would pay for their time on Earth by ascending with the planet when they were ready together. Humanity would also respect and protect the planet at all times, in gratitude for their new home.

At the moment, humanity has not kept their side of the contract. They did not look after their home planet; they were not ready to ascend with Earth and missed the date. The other species were ready and ascended with her. Ascension is going up a significant vibrational level. When playing a computer game and a player goes up a level, the game has not ended but it is played at the higher level and under slightly different circumstances. Right now the Earth, together with the other species that ascended with her, is a big ball of light, paused with a rope ladder dangling down to humanity. Can you reach it and climb up? They will wait as long as there is forward progress towards your own ascension, but not forever.

In 2012 the Earth was reborn and started a new cycle. September 2015 saw a step up, or ascension of the Earth with its guests to a new level. There was chagrin in the human soul when they realised they had failed to be ready and knew they needed some fundamental changes. They had to get serious, to respect and protect the planet and speed up a game that was bogged down with slow, careful learning. Karma was the first casualty of the new rules: it was too slow.

Karma was present on the Earth before 2012, and absent thereafter. Karmic learning allows you to grow through experience. If you murder someone you will live enough lifetimes to understand how that affects people. You will be murdered yourself, be the spouse of the victim, the parent, the child, the sibling, etc. until you have lived through every part and move ahead to learn another lesson. After 2012, humanity had to speed up the game. How to do this in safety? There are almost eight billion souls on Earth right now and events are rocketing forward. If there is no longer any karma what is happening?

One of the major changes to human life on the planet was the demise of the old Earth in the blink of an eye in 2012 as it was reborn in its new form as a higher vibrational planet. To you it looks exactly the same as it always did, but it does not feel the same to the other life forms here. You now have living on Earth people who are unsuited to the planet's higher energy, they simply are not able to connect with the energy of the Earth as it is now. This is crucial for the well-being of the individual, if they are not suited to their environment it means they are living solely on the energy of the food they eat. Those who are plugged into the Earth's energy, such as all the animals and some humans, have their energy boosted by the Earth. It runs through their bodies like an electric current and it increases the energy they have available for their daily lives. It also balances them and as the Earth's energy rises towards the light these people rise effortlessly with her. They spend time outside as much as possible. They are grounded and her energy flows up their legs.

Most of these people don't realise they are on a new Earth, but they are mindful of how their actions affect the planet. They are also interested in protecting the planet and reducing their personal carbon-footprint. Those who were enamoured of their lives, money and power did not take the opportunity to go with the new Earth when she was created.

The people who are running out of life energy are able to continue living on Earth by convincing others to donate their energy to them. This is the sole purpose of large rallies, where crowds are whipped up to provide energy that is siphoned off for the speakers. It works also if a newspaper manipulates its readership to generate anger or fear, or if social media whips up a storm of controversy. The energy is there to be used by others. If you want your energy for yourself, practice loving your neighbour. That energy is impossible to misuse.

There are many, many people on Earth who are empty of energy and are fading. They look just like you but do not have your life force. When they die, they are not coming back but will wait within the greater human soul group until the entire soul ascends, and will not return to Earth to cause any more damage. They don't belong on the new Earth. Those who continue to reincarnate are the ones who chose to go with the planet in 2012, and all the babies that have been born since that time.

4

How Does Ascension Happen?

HUMANITY ran into trouble immediately from the very beginning of your days on Earth. Learning was such a slow process there was no real forward movement for the human race. We angels began to teach about life and felt we had a lot of success in the Atlantean archipelago where people were stationary rather than nomadic. We hot-housed the people of Atlantis and they grew in skill and science. It was a serious drawback that they could see only the three dimensions of height, width and depth, as all other dimensions were hidden from them, including the vast arrays of angels of light or darkness. Our demonic brother angels managed to corrupt the Atlanteans and we were forced into taking emergency action that destroyed Atlantis just in the nick of time. (We wrote about what happened then in our book *The Downfall of Atlantis*).

In later days, following the final battles at the time of King Arthur, there was a change in the way humans learned about themselves. Karma was introduced to slow down the influence of both the light and dark and give people more time to notice when something was shifting to the dark side. People had a better chance to resist what was dark in the world by living with the consequences of their actions. Life settled down with Karma and once again forward progress was slow. (Arthur's story is in *The Downfall of Atlantis*). Somehow there were always a few people who understood in their hearts that you were all one and that you were all a tiny piece of God. These became the Ascended Masters and Mistresses who joined together after death to help and guide those on a spiritual path.

We angels were not idle and continued to offer guidance to those who can hear us and those who are prepared to listen and act on our advice. We are doing the same work on Earth as the Ascended Masters by pointing people along their paths and helping those who are willing to accept guidance. There is no point in working with those who are deaf to us. You have almost eight billion people on your planet and we work directly with only about five thousand of you. If five thousand people walk forward towards the light in their actions and words, others will follow. Someone needs to lead the way and humanity must all be of one mind and purpose by the end of your stay on Earth in order to ascend.

At this point you may feel that five thousand people aren't very many to lead humanity to ascension. Ascension will be like running a marathon where a few are the fastest to cross the finishing line with a great many following behind who are just pleased to complete the race. In this race every runner will receive the same prize, at the same time, on the day the greater human soul ascends. This is something we all hope to see happen within the next hundred years or so, after about five thousand of the fastest learners have crossed an imaginary line and ascend as individuals. They will achieve this in completely different, unique ways. They've been living unique lives and have unique qualities and talents, offering a different example to each of those who watch and follow. These leaders are showing the way across the line by their manner of living every day.

Something else that is helping during this human marathon is that the first over the line create an energetic flow that makes it easier for each of those following to cross the line themselves. As they study and learn about life they set an example and in their turn they pull others along behind them. This creates a steady flow towards ascension. Of course, there needs to be a flow to achieve this; if the energy became stagnant all forward movement would cease. So much of this story is about energy and movement. Ascension itself is full of energy, a giant leap off a spring board landing at a higher level and continuing to learn.

Crossing the line into ascension will bring complete union with the ranks of Ascended Masters and Mistresses. These souls have learned that you are all one, and then united into something like a single diamond. Each facet of the polished diamond shows you the face of a different Master, but inside they are unified. This is where humanity is heading, binding together almost eight billion splinters back into the original soul. You will become one and ascend together, even the people you may not like very much right now. At the end all will go together or none will go.

This may sound like it could take forever! Eight billion souls into one! We watched and waited to see what plan humanity would come up with, knowing that you don't have forever. You are puffing along at the end of a marathon where every other species on the planet has stepped across the line and combined into one great soul without you. Their next experience will be as part of a mega-soul; what will they learn through that experience? You are supposed to be a part of it, they want you to hurry up and join them. They are only prepared to wait if they think you have a chance of arriving and ascending, not if you are wandering around aimlessly on Earth. They waited to see what plan you would come up with to finish this experience and join them.

5

Religion and Afterlife

HEAVEN in Christianity is reserved for a tiny few. It is a vaguely described eternal life where everyone wishes to go and spend eternity with the Creator Who Loves Us All. After all, the opposite is portrayed as hell, purgatory, or for some nothingness, a desolation of existence as one is excluded for eternity from God's presence. Fortunately there is no exclusion from God, ever.

Take yourself back many years ago to the time when truth was forgotten, when an increasingly cluttered society began to lose its simplicity. As people forgot the cycle of life and death, they had to search for a plausible description of what happens next. The bodies of their loved ones were empty of life and that animating soul spark. Where was that soul now? Many variations on what happens next began to be put forward and most of them did not include any further lives on Earth in a physical body. A person had a life, and when it was over there was an afterlife in spirit. God loves you and will take you to heaven or God will torment you forever in hell. This is a particularly unpleasant lie created by man.

The world religions were created by man to make sense of the biggest life event they could see around them, their eventual death and separation from everything they loved. Even after they forgot the circle of life they could not believe there was no afterlife. There couldn't just be this one life spent learning who one was, then have it vanish into nothing. People started to worry about what happened after death and made up different narratives. Religions began to increase in number. There was enough memory of the Golden Rule to "treat others the way you would like to be treated yourself" to include this good and moral behaviour in many religions. Man added the next step of punishing those who misbehaved, whether intentionally or not. "If we can't catch you in this life we'll make sure you're punished in the next!" The good and acceptable people needed to be rewarded in an afterlife of varying descriptions and God would be able to tell who had lived a good life and reward them in paradise.

Living on Earth has always included punishment for contravening established rules of behaviour. It's a bit crude, but it's an effective way to teach children and control those adults who keep hurting others. It has given you opportunities to learn how to show love and compassion to those who do not demonstrate love back to you. Everyone is different and has a different way of learning. Those who hurt others came back to be hurt themselves. In the end karma would have taught every lesson there is to everyone here. All punishment is self-punishment, aimed at providing more opportunities for learning. If you had understood that in your future lives you would redress your wrongs by making sure you suffered what you handed out to others, you may have slowed down and thought about your actions more. Karmic learning was either forgotten or misremembered by a few religions. Even karma began to be perceived as simply providing punishment.

How did this affect humanity's development on Earth? There was a sharp jump in fear among people. Fear is a low vibrational energy and it doesn't matter where on Earth fear starts, it always spreads rapidly. We angels see a world of fear as a world being covered with a blanket of darkness. This bright and shining planet was becoming harder to see as her light became shrouded in fear, the blanket became thicker and denser as religions added ever more restrictions on who could go to heaven.

You mustn't think of religions as deliberately trying to mislead or trick people into beliefs they know are false. Although there are examples of peddling beliefs to make money out of followers, this was never the purpose behind most religions. They were not designed to cause harm, but rather to bring comfort and help shepherd their followers towards the promised happy afterlife. They retained a moral core of good works that helped people live together in greater peace and fairness. The questions of who is God and what does He want from you have been discussed in great depth for millennia by religious leaders. Religions have also been the cause of many wars and acts of cruelty.

Today religion is no longer the simple bringer of comfort, reassuring people that they have a purpose in life and that they are never abandoned by God. The largest religions have splintered in a way that would have been inconceivable one hundred years ago. They have been able to do this because people seem to have lost their ability to know what is true or false. Truth is an aspect of light, and lies are an aspect of darkness - they feel different. In the past it was more common to hear someone say "something there didn't feel right, so I left." Truth and lies are felt in the gut.

6

The Role of Religion on Earth

RELIGIONS are a direct expression of the belief that life itself is not pointless. Why do most people believe that there is more to life, and strive to be the best person they can be and as kind as possible to others? They can feel the existence of their eternal soul. There are always exceptions to this, the power-hungry and criminals who care only for themselves while harming others' peace and happiness. How do these people see their chances of a paradisiacal afterlife? That depends on the promises made by their religions. Mainly religions create a structure and rules to follow to find paradise at the end of life. These rules can be contradictory and contribute to the general confusion, but people hang on to what they learned in their own religion. Their religious organisations are attempting to explain the rules of life to guide them to the best afterlife and avoid eternal torment. The people are searching for meaning to their lives, and acknowledge the spirit within.

All of you are aware of your soul or spirit within, it is ever present in your lives. The only people who deny their spirit are those who believe they do not have one and have put it in a box outside their knowledge and daily life. We find this incomprehensible but then we are not physical, only spirit. Humanity designed a game where it was blindfolded and not told about their eternal spirit, only aware of this one life. When someone insists there is no after life it's a form of brainwashing, and when someone is brainwashed it is always useful to look around and see who benefits. If dark angels, or demons, can convince you that life is meaningless and solely down to chance events, then they have successfully started you down a dark pathway.

If at the end of life there is nothing, then it doesn't matter what you do. You don't have to refrain from hurting others. All things considered, we prefer all those good people in church congregations seeking to know their God and how to live better lives.

Members of churches of every religion are seekers after spirit. We see them earnestly studying and praying, we approve the goal, but in many cases not the teachings or the teachers. Religions have proved too useful for controlling the masses through fear and have little remaining integrity. People who are afraid are easily manipulated for political reasons and gain. Frequently the promises made and teachings are contradictory, but that can be very hard for the members to recognise. You do not need anyone to show you the path to God, you only need to look into your heart where your soul resides

Your individual soul is a vast, wise being. If you were to try to squeeze your entire soul into your own physical body you would only manage to fit a tiny bit of it inside. The rest is always present, but the part you can access easily is the bit you have downloaded into your physical body and energy fields. One of the things you will notice about spiritual teachers is that they often have more of their soul downloaded so the information they learned in previous lives is more available to them. Meditation is a good way for you to bring forward this information into the conscious mind.

Today you, who are a wise being with knowledge from many lifetimes of learning, cannot remember why you are on Earth. That's how it's supposed to be, that is why you are here at all, to try to remember who you are even though you were born with no memory of previous lives. You are searching for clues (this book is a clue) to lead you to the relevant answer and your personal ascension. You are here to first work towards the knowledge that you are one with all humanity, to know it completely and *live* as if you are all one. Once that is realised the second step is knowing you are one with all of creation, including God. As we've written before, if the Creator is a beach made up of trillions of grains of sand, then you can visualise humanity as a grain of sand. There is joy in the Oneness of existence, beginning with the single atom that exploded to create all life in the universe. We like to think of God tossing that atom out and watching the mayhem that resulted. Way back then we were all in that one atom and you are related to absolutely everything.

If you had a physical body but no soul, you would have an empty body, devoid of life. Those who teach life ends at death have an unacknowledged soul, it's there animating their lives but ignored. They believe there is no progress or learning about spirituality, only in keeping a physical body alive with food and drink. There are many such people on your planet today and we feel they have given up on a whole, well-rounded life out of confusion. We don't feel that these people contribute to the learning and forward motion of the human race. In the search for spirituality they are small anchors dragging and slowing down progress. It's the work of this age to remember spiritual truths (Who am I?, Why am I here?, Who is God?), and reject any false teachings. Angels are beings of spirit and we are here to help.

Life begins in spirit, as life eternal as part of the Creator Who Loves Us All. For a long time in our books we referred to this being as the Creator as the love for us was so evident we were comfortable with the shorter name. But this book is for humanity, and we see you exist in a poverty of love where there could be abundance, an endless supply of love to warm your hearts. You have forgotten what a universe full of love can feel like, even when you are suspended in its warm embrace. It barely seems to reach you on Earth, blocked as it is by fear.

The eternal spirit that exists inside the Creator has gifted a spark of life to each living being in the universe. All life has the same source of immortality, your soul is as eternal as the original spirit of God. It is the difference between a living being and a corpse, the clearest demonstration of life and death. You have within you a tiny part of God and when you die you can't lose it because it is you. It is your connection to the Creator and everything that has ever been created, seen and unseen. God spread Himself out and made many universes, which will forever be part of Him just as you are part of him.

7

Theories of Reincarnation

HAVE WE convinced you that you have an immortal soul, that when this body ends the most important part of you will carry on? In a way your soul flows like a ribbon through the universe, meeting some people here, then twisting and flowing away to join others over there; a ribbon of gold energy touching the lives of other people, other animals, new locations. You touch down lightly for a while and absorb knowledge, then lift and flow away. Others are doing the same and your paths cross many times, in many places. You make patterns, sometimes elegant woven patterns of light, then they alter and flow away again. Life moves effortlessly and you find yourself always in the right place with the right companions. What at first seems unplanned and pointless always happens exactly as it should. Life is variable, effortless and pleasurable. Then you are born into a body.

The life of spirit just described could be replicated in your physical life on Earth, if only you were able to enjoy flowing between people and events as you do in spirit! You could do this if you dared, but an ever-changing existence is rarely the way life is lived here. There are reasons of course why you are not all flowing from place to place during your lives. Human society has not yet worked out a way to accommodate this. There are many who feel stuck or trapped in jobs, marriages or unhealthy bodies. This is the opposite of light and flow. You are living a stagnant and dark existence that comes from fear and breeds even more fear. Any stuck situation is an expression of darkness, not the love and light that is available to you. It slows and muddies the energy.

We encourage you to stop resisting change, longing for a vanished past up to the point where you no longer work for your futures together. In some places we see a walk towards the light, in some others a swarming about with no movement in any direction, and in a few other places it's a picture of an elbows-linked line of people trying to hold everyone behind them in place, and if possible take backwards steps. What will happen in these places will be like a dam bursting as the elbows are pushed apart and everyone pours through. But for now the line is holding as the crowd behind builds up strength. The strongest force in the universe is change and that leads to flow, and flow is an aspect of light and love. Change is the first step towards light.

Change tends to inspire fear in many people and this fear is cultivated by those that thrive on darkness. It's how the armaments industry is kept so buoyant as many feel the need to protect themselves from the unfamiliar. People fear the great unknown, going where they have no previous memory and dying with no real idea of what happens to their soul. Being taught you will be in paradise is supposed to help, but that's too vague. Those who temporarily die on a hospital bed talk about a tunnel of light, not a paradise they don't want to leave. So the afterlife is not really known, there are few accepted first hand reports of people coming and going besides the tunnel. It remains frightening and a mystery.

There are societies that look at a person and judge them on their past lives by looking at their present life. "They must have done something bad to be born to lowly parents, they are being punished in this life for a previous life." They make the punishment stick by making sure they don't move out of the position they were born in. In some religions those who reincarnate as non-human must have done something even worse. They are short-lived insects or animals, not even good enough to be human anymore. The transmigration of souls is a religious teaching that is false. We won't say it never happens that human souls return as a non-human, but only those who have mastered their human form come back at times as an animal. A human Ascended Master can choose to return to Earth and help in animal form with that animal's higher consciousness's permission, but it is very rare. Whales and dolphins are the most frequent, but not the only, choices. That does not make them superior to the whales and dolphins that do not have human souls. From their point of view of timeless ascendancy they can see where to go to assist life on the planet. We appreciate the help!

Human body, whale body - flowing from one into the other then back again to the human soul group. The stagnancy that would forbid this is not part of the universe, it is part of life on Earth. The universe has far more life and flow, stagnancy and darkness than you can imagine. Earth is like a little frozen pea sitting in space, frozen in fear and afraid of moving forward. We write this book to ease your fear.

8

Flowing from Life to Death and Back

WHAT MAKES you the most afraid? For many of you it has been fear and worry about family and money. Fear that at the end of your life you might be living in an incapacitated state and in loneliness, or worried whether you'll go to heaven or not. Some of this is due to the way you live now, separated by distance from your families and children. In the past there were always some people who left home and travelled, that had a drive to see what was beyond the horizon, but there were more who did not leave, forming a little community of extended family and friends in one neighbourhood or town. It is almost a luxury now to have family near by, sharing their love and support. One of the saddest aspects of a world of refugees is the destruction of these family communities through death and exile. Be kind to one another.

Those without family and friends worry about their increasing feebleness as they age and wonder how the years will pass until their deaths. Imagine you are this person and the quiet sadness that is your state of mind. Do you live to be happy or sad? Would you like to say goodbye and leave at the time of your choosing? Think about it, not suicide, but "I'm finished here, my body is so painful and weak and I'm so lonely that I will stop living now. I will wait to return with a new, young body and a new purpose." This is a planned reincarnation without any cultural or social baggage. Take a step from life to death in the knowledge that your eternal soul does not die, only the worn out body. It used to always be that way before people forgot how to die.

Many of you may be thinking you have no idea how to stop living even if you wanted to! And yet, you have heard stories about death, such as a parent waiting to die until all the children were gathered together, even if it took some days to get everyone there. These people are controlling their time of leaving. Surrounded by family they allow everyone to say their goodbyes and soon after they are gone. Others have no idea how to stop living when their time is up, these are the ones who often feel it necessary to contract a painful illness such as cancer because they don't remember any other way to leave. It's not every case of cancer, but it happens a lot. Not everyone incarnates to live to old age, people can have a life plan that includes death at any age. Once a life plan has been completed one can choose to leave and come back again and have a new learning experience. Or they can choose to stay alive and pick a new purpose that interests them and spend more years with their families. They can even stay and not pick a new path, but just live and enjoy themselves.

This is how dying took place for millennia. Because people were closer to understanding their life on this planet, they passed smoothly between life and death and back to life again. They were closer to understanding who they were and what their role here was. When they distanced themselves from Earth by living away from the land, they made a detour down a blind alley. It's time for humanity to turn around and head back, and remember the cycle of living.

When you have sad people in your midst, those who want to leave the planet but are stuck here, they have a damping effect on every single person alive. When you have a joyful person they brighten up the lives of every person. The energy they hold is part of the world environment, your environment. If you have to maintain joy in the face of fear, worry and sadness, it requires strength and determination not to slide into those low vibrations yourself. It's worth the effort, because as we said, are you here to live a happy life or a sad life? The more of you who can project happiness, always looking for the bright side, the easier it becomes for everyone else. It matters a lot what kind of energy you emit. It's what you contribute to the world.

Let's say you are hopeful and people around you are hopeful too. This is the view that things are going to get better and better. People look up more, smile more, and take more risks with their lives. They feel confident that whatever they do will work out well for them, so they get busy. There's excitement and sharing as they use their curiosity to find out what friends are up to and congratulate them. They know they are in the flow of energy and so will be receiving more everytime they let something go. They are therefore generous to those who have less. They feel no lack in the present and certainly not in the future, the future is going to be great! The energy is high, bright and golden.

Contrast that with fear. One of the first acts of the fearful is to hang on tight to everything they have in case they never receive anything more and run out of food and shelter. Risk becomes unattractive, people look down and away so they can't be approached for money or food. Sharing bad luck stories happens, but it makes people feel wretched and sadness spreads. The energy being spread from living in fear is dark and thick and drags everyone down, movement becomes difficult and no one wishes to move in any direction. Too risky.

We can see these pools of fear and darkness on Earth. In some places it is lighter, in a few places on the planet it is bright. Those places are remote and self-sufficient with less contact with others. The upland pastures of the Himalayas look bright. The darkness is thickest in the United States, Europe, and Africa. The dark energy swirls everywhere. In the Himalayas the brightness of the people keeps the darkness at bay.

You live in a darkening world, trying to find your way through a thick black fog of energy. Try to shift your perception, say "I choose to look at the energy of those around me and not just the physical appearance.". To navigate a life through the blackness of this fog is very difficult. The Earth, the stars and the universe itself send wave after wave of light to help you and help the planet. We will never stop trying to help you.

9

A Time of Correction

IT IS FUNDAMENTAL to understanding who you are to first know that you have an individual and immortal soul. To understand that you return to Earth for multiple lives that allow you to learn and give a purpose to your existence and which affects the entire planet with your own vibration of light. This is the starting point on which you base your future life times and learning. If this is understood as given you can unfreeze yourselves and begin moving forward as you did in the past. This lack of understanding was not the fault of any world religions, which were created to answer questions. You originally intended to find the answers for yourself, through those eureka! moments that occur throughout life. Your experience and observation, contemplation and meditation would allow you to teach yourself. You would die one day but your hard-earned knowledge would not die with you, but become part of your soul. It's no where near as bleak a story as a meaningless life. You can start moving forward again with this knowledge and learn as you live, knowing that everything has a value and a meaning.

Today confusion is everywhere on your planet! There has been an explosion of beliefs, and in that explosion some pieces have gone missing. In this we see the energy of fear actively preventing many of you from welcoming the traveller and the stranger into your homes. Yet you know you would wish to be welcomed if you were the traveller. You treat others not with kindness, but with hostility and often see them as worthless. These others then retaliate and the cycle repeats a little faster, a little stronger in vibration. It sets more firmly into your beliefs and experiences, reinforcing a negative outlook as the vibration drops lower and lower because of your actions. Why does this matter? Isn't it possible to learn from the low as well as high? Of course you can. There are many lessons that fear and misery, grief and despair can teach you, but you have learned all of those lessons already. Do you really want to go over this old ground yet again and emerge a step lower on the ladder? Your higher self has already made other plans.

Humanity is a soul of light, wise and ancient. It learned it was a part of the Creator many times in the past through living on different planets. Always the games or learning experiences it devised allowed the entire universe to take a collective step forward. When a soul busy learning on a planet wraps up a game and consolidates it into their soul as part of their own growth, it allows all the souls in the universe to take another step upwards. It's like bubbles in a bath rising higher, each connected to all the bubbles rising together. This is close to how individual human souls rise together, helping each other into the light. What about when the bubbles vanish? This can happen in a universe as easily as in a bath. We are there to help you whip the bubbles up again together with those of you who have worked so hard to find the light. We do not let their progress die away.

The human soul is looking at what it can do to learn the lessons of light and love at this time. These are the vibrations that will take you to your next level and will bring your existence one step closer to the Creator Who Loves Us All. You have known this and always looked for love and happiness in your lives, not despair. Why are so many listening to the voices of hate today? Those who preach hate are many, from politicians, radio talk show hosts, religious leaders and those who are simply afraid of other people. Their fear overwhelms them, they live their lives trying to shut out all but the few people they see as being in agreement with themselves. In order to do this they need to believe the lies they are told that distort the way they see others. You can blame the liars who make the problems worse but there are many who wish to hear the lies to justify their deeply held fears. They are looking for a solution to their fears, so many fears now that they don't remember the original one - what happens after their life on Earth comes to an end.

This is a time of correction to repair the drift that began a long time ago, from knowledge to ignorance and superstition. It began with greed and stratification of societies and with the need to increase personal income and power through the labour of others. Not everyone had to be a farmer or fisherman, but there was a shift to look down on those whose work produced no more income than was necessary. Many built up a life based on the work of others, managing their efforts without fairly sharing with them the profits based on that work. If one despises others then their work is not valued.

The numbers of different people and different jobs on Earth is astonishing. How could anyone expect to be familiar with all of these? We honour each of you, and so honour your honest work. When a person despises another and implies that they are not as good as he is, then he is most likely incapable of imagining himself in their place. He would still have a lot of lessons to learn in understanding and knowledge. This person needs your help and should not be treated with condescension in their turn. It is not an easy task to treat all your fellow humans as you wish to be treated yourself, however, it is a giant leap forward for those who can do this, the final leap to take you past the finishing line. Those who understand and act upon the knowledge that all are one ascend first and lend a helping hand to everyone following behind, extending their hands with love.

Honest work is now rewarded at vastly different levels depending on the profitability of the business, not on its value to humanity (as in banking versus farming.) What you really cannot live without is food and water and yet these people are not always rewarded above subsistence level around the world. We see that ignorance of where food comes from has created a level of disrespect and lack of recompense for those who do this important work. Honouring those workers who serve you by growing your food is paramount and helps you take the next step of honouring many other jobs. Each of you participates in withholding a living wage from some while generously rewarding others, while forgetting you are all one. Each of you needs to care for the other. You are all jointly responsible for the whole of humanity.

Humanity has used its creativity to devise new ways of separating from one another. You may think of a civil war as two sides fighting with weapons. You are living through a civil war between those who hold others in contempt and those who hold others in love. These two sides can often be found in the same households today, battling with ideology and words while the divisions grow deeper and wider. Those who look for personal gain by crushing the other side keep the rhetoric going. If humanity does not come together as one then they will have failed to learn the lessons that they came here to learn: you are all one with each other and all of life in the universe and each of you is a tiny part of God.

10

Steep Decline in Population

THE HARDENING of ideology on the planet today is a dominant theme in politics, and at the same time politicians take decisions that have huge impact on the daily lives of the people in their nations. We can see a level of blindness in these politicians that causes them to do untold harm to their citizens: the simple blindness of failing to observe the effects of their decisions. They are excited by the cut and thrust of the political fray, choosing sides and playing a game as their job, but their games have consequences. The people are saddled not so much with inept men ruling and making decisions, but with systems that have already failed.

In the nations where divisions are hardening the prospects are that they will have sudden changes. Overnight some will stop being democracies, with elections suspended pending the resolution of some crisis. Others will have pockets of rebellion, perhaps that will be the excuse for swift change and military intervention. This has happened many times before to bring about the end of the old and beginning of something new. In the USA, where there are a great number of weapons in the homes of the general public, there is the danger of high casualty levels. All of this will be happening because people are afraid of others, and few recognise the harm they inflict is hurting themselves. They do not feel enough love. The death toll will rise.

This is what we call making changes the hard way, especially in countries where there is no love, empathy or cooperation. It will only change through seeing yourself in others and drawing back from conflict. Because of the raised natural death, rate people will feel they are in a crisis situation that they don't understand. They will look for someone to blame for the deaths and every kind of wild theory will be put forward on social media. To survive this with your heart intact you will have to protect yourself. This can be done by staying in the middle and being a bridge where possible between opposing ideologies. That way you do not add to the problem yourself and you are modelling a different kind of behaviour. There is fault on both sides of every argument and this period of unrest and revolution will cause hardship to many. If you want to step away from it, move your family away from the cities.

If on reading this you think "oh no, not again!" then you are right. This was preventable but it needed earlier action in national and local governments. Responsiveness to the needs of the majority of citizens would have prevented all of what's coming. The cause of this is the subversion of democracy in the West. Patching in changes could help in the short term. Many of you feel like you are faced with a dying planet, early death and hardship as you compete for food, water and jobs. If only there was more abundance and fewer people! How long will it take for the population to rebalance at a level the Earth can support in a healthy and relaxed manner? Is there enough time for this to happen before everyone dies?

We see a steep decline in population over the next decade or two, then there will be stabilisation at a lower level. As the human population level drops there will be less need for petrochemicals to be burned and food to be grown in the areas that used to be for animals. We see a variety of ways that the population will decrease, leaving because their time is up and the decline in the birth rate being the two with the greatest impact. Don't worry about war and pestilence wiping out the human race, that is not your future.

Humanity to us looks like a body running around screaming, lost in confusion of what to do and where to go next. The closer you come to destroying the Earth, the more hopeless people feel. It is the most important thing in the background of their lives. Of all the topics it is the one they wish their governments would address, but the world governments are resisting acknowledging this, not wanting to spend money on finding working solutions. They have turned their backs on the people and their eyes follow the corporate money as it is waved in front of them, hypnotised.

So what is going to happen, how is humanity going to fix this situation or are you going to crash out of this game taking all the other species with you? Not if the greater human soul can help it. The level of change required in population numbers is huge. As national governments stand by and watch the Earth die they will be scrapped if they can not become effective. There will be a turnover inside these governments that will reflect the national death rates. You are entering a period of great change.

Humans are always very resistant to change, yet it is the one constant factor in this universe of change. Once a change has been made it is the new status quo, and that immediately begins to shift into what is coming next. Your short life spans on Earth have helped you move forward by limiting the amount of change you can experience in one lifetime. Embracing change will help on a personal level, also by recognizing that you are now in a situation where corrective change will be a good thing. The timing is correct, and the chance of good results is excellent!

Part Two
The Level Playing Field

11

Partnership With Angels

HUMANITY will be at the point of ascension when everyone treats each other as equals, in personal relationships and in society as a whole. People will no longer attempt to climb the ladder of success without helping others to rise with them at the same speed. When we write about equality of income or position we do not mean everyone has to have exactly the same in life. We do, however, mean that the top and the bottom of society draw closer together. This is the proof that you understand you are all one soul; your actions will reflect this understanding. If you understand that everyone is a part of you and a part of your human family, then demonstrate it by treating others that way. This is always the final step in anyone's understanding, taking the knowledge into your hearts and letting it form your actions.

Taking action is why you are here on Earth, we angels are often quite envious of your power to act. We have many facets to our existence, but our interactions with humanity are centred around guidance and suggestions. We have the agony of watching lovely people walk blindly into trouble and we can't reach out to stop them, we can't make their feet take a different path. If they fall down a deep, dark pit we want to stretch out our hands and help them climb up, but we don't have any hands. We must use our powers of suggestion to guide another human being to the pit, lower a rope and pull them up. These rescuers could be family and friends, or professionals like doctors, nurses and psychologists. We are always looking for people who can hear us so we can work more closely with them.

One of our great advantages when helping humanity is that we know how this game ends, living as we do in the timeless universe. All beginnings and endings are visible to us, it is this knowledge that helps us advise people effectively. We take care of those who see us and listen to us, we guide them to keep them safe and happy. As they grow in spirituality these are the people who seed the Earth with light, light that grows into words and deeds. If all our words lead to nothing, if there is no resulting action, then we must begin again and find another way or another person.

In the past we worked with individuals of many different skills and abilities. We found men who were prophets and preachers. Men who were listened to by other men. We found women who listened and acted on the words they heard by bringing the teachings into their families and communities. We found men more at ease in putting themselves in the centre of crowds and speaking loudly, and women better at taking action. It's important to remember that you are one with every man and every woman, that all have different gifts to bring to any situation. It's unusual to find a woman who can shout over a crowd without amplification and for most of your time here amplification did not exist. Talking to smaller groups worked well in the past for women. We do not value one sex over the other, we see you each gifted with a different set of talents and want to see you make the best of what you have been given. You chose your sex before you incarnated for this lifetime and you have lived many lives in both sexes. So we wonder at the willingness now of both sexes to walk separate lives, suspicious of each other's motives and actions.

Some men still treat women as smaller and weaker prey, there is no love in this, or acknowledgement that you are all one.

In the beginning of this universe, humanity was created as a single soul with one mind and spirit. You proceeded to arrange with a willing planet to incarnate and live with physical bodies to learn about what it is to be a tiny part of God. Humanity's single soul divided into individual pieces to learn more quickly at the same time. You set up rules and parameters and proceeded to reside on the planet until you learned who you were and who God is. Then humanity arranged with a new planet to live and learn again with slightly different rules, separating into bodies once more. This has happened many times during the lifetime of this universe. Between each planetary game humanity recombined into its true self, one single soul, wiser than before. This is the soul present on Earth now, that you are each a tiny part of. When we keep saying "you are all one" we mean there is only one soul and you are a fraction of it. It's a reflection of the way the physical human body is made up of many cells, each cell being a necessary part of the whole and each cell of equal value.

Humanity seems to have completely forgotten its unity and purpose, the evidence for this is perpetual warfare. If this was the human body with organs and cells at war with each other you would die. Hopefully before that happened you would seek help from a healer or doctor and we angels are here to help your soul survive. We do this because when you travel ever farther back into the beginnings of this universe, we were one with you. We accept that we are splinters of an even greater soul and we will always work to save any part of it that is weak and in danger of collapse. We help all those who are reaching for the light in the universe and from the very beginning we have played this role.

Angels have not evolved in wisdom and knowledge by incarnating on planets in physical bodies, although there are individual exceptions to this rule. We grow by watching and helping others and we are beings of great sensitivity and feeling. Your pain is our pain, your joy is our joy. We are beings of light, love, truth and joy. We are able to sense your pain quite acutely and it makes us feel compassion for you. We exert ourselves continually in our efforts to guide you towards the light that we align with. We accept that we can suggest, but not manipulate or demand. Our guidance often takes the form of dreams and coincidences, whispers in your ears and bringing people closer for you to meet in the ordinary course of your day. Watch for these dreams and these chance meetings, be more aware of your conversations. Some meetings have great depth, an exchange of information and ideas to send you both away changed in your view of the world. We need to help people to stop hurting each other and this comes from inside you. Then the vibration around that person changes, altering the entire soul group. It can be slow work; how much time now does humanity have left on Earth?

We are leaning rather heavily on the few people who listen to us and are active on our behalf. They are growing in wisdom and knowledge as they work with us, many of them correctly seeing this as an opportunity for personal ascension. Our Earthly helpers see others as sisters and brothers and they have compassion for them. They look into another's eyes and see themselves looking back and refuse to harm them; they do not fail to help them. They see how they overlap with all people and barely see themselves as individuals. In this lifetime they have become ready to rejoin their soul group as one of the Ascended Masters and Mistresses. From there they can chose: either another life or to stay in spirit as guides for those on Earth.

Ascended Masters and Mistresses have been continuously created over the years. Even in difficult times a few people have always managed to relearn that they are a tiny part of God. We expect this process of personal ascension to quicken. As it accelerates the balance changes more quickly inside the soul. If the percentage of ascended individuals increases, the soul has a greater proportion of light. It changes the way choices are made inside the greater human soul and the choices become more knowledgeable and enlightened. Humanity becomes more determined to end the slide into darkness and remain a soul of light. It sees the pace of change accelerate and, instead of slowing it down, makes choices that help the soul keep up and ascend. One of its main threads of action right now is to help as many as possible keep pace with the Earth's changes.

This is a time of acceleration, and those who work with us have woven themselves into the prevailing energy. The best way to keep up with the Earth is to spend time outside and the wilder the area the better. A woodland is more beneficial than a sports field. The Earth is accelerating into her next phase, she is raising her vibration daily to arrive at the level she needs to be at for a change to a new direction.

We know that because you are human you automatically think that going forward is usually ahead, a straight line on paper, a straight road or straight up in the air. This is not what happens when a planet exists in space where straight ahead is irrelevant. She will be moving ahead at a new angle, like following a road that suddenly takes a turn. Her vibration is not lifting up from one level to the next, it is humming a new tune. There will be a different quality to it. If you were singing a song and picked a new base rhythm such as rumba or hip-hop you would feel the difference. Your body would want to move in a different way. Your planet is making the adjustments she needs to for her next phase and this will be a livelier rhythm. What will this mean to Earth and her guests?

12

The Turning Point

RHYTHM is as much a part of the universe as all other expressions of energy. It gives character to your spoken dialects, poetry and music. It is the background sound to your lives and begins with the heartbeat of the Earth and from there the rhythm travels up to the surface to where the Earth resonates with sound energy from the 1-2-3 beat of the American desert to the oom-pah band sound of the Alps. You rely on this steady beat as it helps you keep time and supports you with its familiarity. You have lived for decades with this particular rhythm forming the background, the energy establishing a mood. It is a clockwork beat, one that you could march to, the modern dance form of body-popping draws on this energy.

There is always a rhythm to life and some are better at hearing it than others. These people tend to be more relaxed and accepting of the ebbs and flows that occur in their lives. They are more grounded into their environments, less stressed. Then there are all of those who push on and ignore every rhythm from day length, seasonal, diurnal, menstrual, etc. This is not entirely sensible or sustainable. You pay a price for ignoring your environment, it is stressful for you to pretend every day is the same.

What's the next Earth change? Imagine people moving sedately on a dance floor, with controlled and measured movements. Not very exciting, but not standing still, either. What is the new rhythm? Welcome to Planet Disco! Turn down the lights, set the mirror ball turning and shine the coloured lasers! The Earth has changed the music and set a new beat, an irregular one you can't march to. It's time to loosen up and party! The measured steps and rules you all obey will be out of synch, they will begin to jar and be difficult to enforce unless they fit the rhythm. It is time to let some of them go, keeping only those that fit the underlying beat. These rules will be easy to live with and enforce. This particular rhythm change creates a mood of celebration and joy, a time to let the fear and sadness drop out of your lives. There is always someone in the universe reaching out a helping hand to humanity, this time it is the Earth.

This is music to enjoy yourself with, moving in any direction with random dance steps. It is unpredictable, and no one cares anymore. Everyone has to move to the rhythm they feel coming up through their feet into their bodies. Some will take longer to notice than others, it depends how good they are at ignoring the planet. Some will find this very, very uncomfortable energy. They will find it hard to live like this and be shaken to their core.

What does it mean for humanity after this Earth-change? It will help people take a look at what's happening in an area of life and decide to walk away. If a politician tries to engage a crowd with their rhetoric and persuade them to follow where they lead, they'll find they're talking to an empty room. No one will want to stay and listen to what they're saying. They look out a window to where everyone is enjoying themselves on the grass and start to think they should go outside and join them too. We have written about this phenomenon in our previous books, the point where people turn and walk away from the status quo. This is one of those turning points.

You are at the point of change right now, which will lead to the status quo altering in a few years. What is the current situation on Earth? There are a few families with a great deal of money and possessions, wielding power solely in their own interests. There are too many people who don't have enough to eat or who are not able to live joyful lives free of worry. There is a great overbalance towards worry and fear. The few who enjoy their lives can't redress the energetic balance. They have created a world where there is too little joy for everyone, including themselves. We wrote in our previous book *Stepping Through the Looking Glass* that love and joy are the diamonds and gold of the universe. We are here to help the greater human soul find love and joy, that is why we continue to help through suggestion and guidance.

This will all change for humanity in the near future. It is a way of living that has run its course and even though it is still present on Earth it is diminishing energetically. Everything in existence needs energy to sustain it, like filling up an empty balloon. Even an economic system needs energy to carry on, when the energy has shifted away to something else the system will collapse as a new one takes off. It is a fact of life in this universe that energy ebbs and flows and nothing ever stays the same.

How might your economies and social structures change? We see it happening fast, in the manner of a bowling ball hitting the pins at the end of the alley. The ball smacks into the pins and they go flying off in different directions. Everyone cheers at a solid hit! We see your pins sitting in positions of power and authority, not all governmental or corporate, but also religious and ideological. There are organisations such as, for example, the National Rifle Association in the USA, which affect the lives of others far beyond their membership. This organisation holds an ideology they refuse to change for any reason. When pushed, they resist any movement and hold their space in society even tighter. As times change around them they have an opportunity to change and become what is needed in the debate around gun control. They could be fluid and flowing, not following, but leading the changes. Or they can continue to dig in and try to block any proposals for change. Smack! The force of change is strong enough to hit them and send them flying. By sitting still they make themselves a stationary target.

When an immovable object is met by an irresistible force the object will move. You will see this over and over again in the next few years. The object being moved will be devoid of energy, empty of light, finished and ready to be swept away. There will be confusion about what is happening and we want you to remember this guidance so you may navigate around the surprises. Those of you who have picked up this book are already sensitive to energy even if you are untrained. You can stop, think and feel what is going on. If you have employment you may be worried about its security. We're saying that if you stop and focus on where you work and what type of place it is you will know what to do. You can base your decisions on your instincts, they rarely let you down. The same goes for where you live, where you keep your savings, etc. Not everyone you meet in daily life can do this, but you can.

13

The Energy of Social Media

A S EVERYTHING begins to change we want you to enjoy the process. Your soul group is orchestrating it for the highest good of all beings of light. Your higher self is part of the driving force behind this, because once you reach the end of a game such as this, you have finished it, there is no more to be learned here. You go on to another situation and learn something new. If you invest emotionally, financially and energetically in trying to continue a situation that has ended you are spending yourself in a lost cause. Why not look for the prevailing direction of change and explore the new path? You will step onto a pathway that is full of strong, new energy, like stepping out of a ruined city into one that is beautiful and alive with people. You came to learn about being human, to learn everything you possibly could through living. That is not by existing and giving your energy to something or someone that had the same chances to learn that you did, but failed. Their turn has ended.

You have among you on your planet today the walking dead, those who are only here by siphoning off energy from others. They are not aware they are doing this, just as their donors are unaware. They have never been asked if they are happy to give up their life force to keep these people alive. Be aware of who you give your energy to, you don't have to be in their presence to provide the type of energy they need, it can be on social media. When you turn the other cheek it removes your energy from a situation. Don't pour it away into disagreements. Social media can be used as an energy funnel; hatefulness and rage will feed some people, happy sharings feed a different set. The energy is created and used, there is not a limit on the amount of hate or love that can be created and both spread quickly. If you contribute to hateful arguments you help grow hate on your planet. If you withdraw from these arguments and instead contribute love somewhere else, you create ever more love. Consciously choose which of these you wish to create. In the beginning these global social media sites were an amazing way to connect everyone and help people get to know others better. It can still be used that way, but be careful of what you give your energy to online.

There is a division growing between neighbours and friends on ideological grounds. This is also fuelled by online social contact. Your neighbours are more like you than many other people, you have more in common with your fellow citizens than people living on the other side of the world. The divisions between you are small and you would know this if you spent more time with them face to face in social interaction. Use your social sites to arrange personal meet-ups, rediscover how much you are alike as members of a single soul. Look for ways to turn the other cheek whether others have learned how to do this or not. It's hard to keep fighting when everyone else has turned away.

Many of the ideological arguments have their roots in fear and anger and can be felt in a very personal way. Those who are angry usually feel they have a reason for this. So much of this anger has it basis in lies and manipulation and as beings of truth we see this very clearly. We don't want readers to jump to the conclusion that others are stupid or gullible. There is such a massive and pervasive quagmire of lies weaving throughout your lives that you are all affected. You all believe some untruths and it is very hard to get to the bottom of the important stories of your time. Or it was.

14

Climate Change

EVERYTHING is changed and light is growing from above and below. The secrets buried in the deepest cellars are being illuminated by light rising from the Earth and some people see what is hidden there and are asking questions. Light is coming down from the universe itself in many forms. Much of this appears to come from the Sun, we are using her as a relay station for energy from other stars. She sends it out in solar flares and different bands of radiation, as well as daylight. The Central Sun of your galaxy is concentrating on sending energy to Earth and her Sun right now; she is the top galactic priority at this time and is being given a helping hand. Stars and planets work together for the same goal.

We wish you could see the energy zinging towards your Earth right now. If you feed a lot of energy into a planet in this way she grows and develops. She is making great progress with her own plan of remembering who she is as a tiny part of God and this energy helps every living being on her surface. We can see flowing lines of energy, much of it pink, being triangulated through other stars and planets and targeted to her. When energy passes through stars and planets it picks up a quality of their energy, before turning a corner and being sent on to Earth. They are helping her to remember her family, the universe and her place in this moving tapestry. The last time she was energised in this way they were all sitting in different locations in space in relation to her. The universe has moved around and she is learning about her place again. This happens from time to time and before it was Earth's turn it was the turn of a different planet.

In addition to learning where she is now in a multi-dimensional tapestry, Earth is being gifted with energy, receiving an extra push along her path. Whatever happens next she will be on course. She is changing, and she contributes to the recent climate change along with humanity. If humanity had not altered the climate, the changes would be steadier and less damaging. The wild swings and dangerous weather is from humans, she would not have needed to produce extreme change to get where she wanted to go. It doesn't help her to have extreme weather, she has to work around it in order to progress. Earth healing groups are working to steady her for everyone's benefit and they could use some help from everyone who is interested in this important work.

A long time ago the Earth went through a similar series of changes in preparation for the next phase of development. She has learned and progressed by hosting others on the surface. In the past she reached a level where it felt like she was stretching larger than her skin, when her soul's vibration had raised and she felt her body was heavy and solid, she needed a lighter body to house a soul carrying more light. She folded in as a flower does at dusk, ready to open the next morning in all its beauty again. She re-opened looking almost the same, but the colours were more pure and the petals were stronger and less likely to bruise and spoil. During the folding-in she ended all life on her surface and started afresh with a new set of beings, each with new contracts. The old contracts had finished and those souls moved on somewhere else before she changed to a higher vibration.

This time it is trickier for her to renew herself in the same way she did before. She had planned her own evolution by incorporating all the other souls present here into a multi-soul ball of light. The souls of light would be stronger when combined together than as separate individual beings. Included are plants, animals, insects, bacteria, minerals and more, each with its own soul. The Earth's next leap forward was planned long in advance when she contracted to take all of these beings onboard for games of their own design. The fee for their stay here was to join her in ascension. If God is a beach and you are a grain of sand, then joining into one large soul could be compared to sand being melted by a lightening strike, turning the sand into glass. It is still on the beach, but it now it has a greater size. One day the entire beach will be drawn back into God as one, and the Earth signals the start of that swift process by combining with others in this way.

There is a hitch in the plan in that humanity has almost learned who they are once more but not quite finished their game. You are going over the last few lessons again to make sure everything is learned, and the current divisiveness demonstrates the backwards travel in society today. The Earth, combined with all the other souls, is ready to fold in and open out into a new, massive flower. She'll go from being a tiny blossom to a large sunflower overnight, and she will shine.

15

Finding Your Balance

WHAT CAN YOU expect from the Earth while she is in this holding pattern? She had planned to alter her climate to set up the next phase of her existence. Now she is challenged by the turbulence of manmade climate change layered on top of her designs. She wished to release seismic tension gradually in smaller bursts, but now she is pushed to let it off in larger volcanic events, earthquakes, tsunamis and floods in an attempt to stabilize herself. The winters are becoming colder and wetter, while the summers are hotter and dryer in many parts of the world. All of this alters the environment for a large number of her surface guests. She cares for all life and is attempting to remain stable and make changes safely, this is now proving difficult and she needs your help. Earth healing was always part of the human contract with the planet. Instead there is toxic activity like pollution and fracking. When we say humanity is going over the last few lessons again to make sure everything is learned before ascension, taking care of your planet is one of those lessons.

Earth healing today is about balance. This is one area in which you are able to help her, lessening the wild swings and becoming more settled. She is receiving waves of energy from the universe, all planned eons ago and sent on their way. Today she may have chosen to arrange these flows of energy differently, instead of a zingy type of energy giving her little pushes forward, she may have chosen balancing and calming waves. You can help her by being balanced yourself.

A balanced person is neither light nor dark, but is both. Everyone has a dark side to go with their light side, as does the Creator. Everything the Creator has created has come from inside of Him, He is light and dark blended together. This is what it is, in essence, to be whole. To become whole is to acknowledge that light and dark are both part of your make-up, and then your behaviour shows your personal choices. Even the most enlightened human can remember a time when they did something they are not proud of. If you acknowledge it and own it as your own behaviour and not someone else's then you are seeing yourself as a whole being. You all desire to become as you once were, a tiny part of God, and this means being a whole person again.

Most people are somewhat whole and balanced, think of all the billions of people who have their own lives and families, neighbourhoods and jobs. They have to combine all the parts of their lives so that these parts end up creating a balance. They are like a wagon wheel with many spokes reaching away from the centre creating something rounded and whole. If one spoke was too long or too short, or missing altogether, they would not be balanced and would find life a little harder. If they are part of a community there would be help for them as the larger unit can absorb smaller imbalances and still remain whole.

The community can remain balanced and on its feet while the imbalances are accommodated. It is done by looking after the elderly or infants, the blind, deaf or the disabled. Making room for others is one way of living with love and with peace in your hearts. This makes up a balanced society.

Many of you feel that you are doing your best to live a balanced life in a crazy, complicated world. You walk upright in a steady way, moving ahead with your family and at about every step someone else loses their balance and crashes into you, pushing you to your knees. You feel surrounded by people who surely can not be in their right minds! They show signs of mental distress and illness, they have physical diseases caused by stress and have harried, unbalanced lives. Children rarely see their parents and there is so much sadness and separation everywhere. They are all doing the best they can in difficult circumstances.

The underlying imbalance on this planet seeping into your societies is that you don't remember who you are and that your neighbour is a part of you. They are the cell-next-door, if we use the human body as an analogy of wholeness. Only by denying your kinship with all others can one person prey on another, and this is done in so many ways. In this modern age it can be through taking people's money or just the chance to live a happy life.

You fend off all the people, corporations and governments that are trying to extract money from you every day. Do angels care about money? Not really, but on your planet it carries the energy of exchange. You use it to store the value of your labour. If you work for a farmer in the summer you could be paid in vegetables, but they would be rotted by the middle of winter. Money allows you to spread out the energy of your labour. It means a great deal to you because you worked for it. When it is taken from you and spent by others who did not earn it you feel robbed. You become emotionally unbalanced and feel like the world you live in is broken.

It's this broken world and broken society that upsets the balance. Yet there doesn't seem to be a plan to fix it, or no one has any idea how to fix the world and it keeps getting new patches applied that seem to be the wrong patches. This is up to humanity to repair, to put right anything they have done that harms themselves or another species. You hold in yourself a kernel of the larger human soul, your role includes correcting what has gone wrong in the past. You have the physical presence here, the body and hands to take action. This is why you are here now, why others stood aside and let you join the front of the line to be born again on Earth. All of you here know this and doing what you came here to do is incredibly satisfying. Anytime you disagree with someone on how to put everything right there is a sure-fire answer that will work to solve everything. Love your neighbour as yourself, treat you neighbour the way you would like to be treated yourself.

16

Using the Infinity Loop to Balance

WE RECOMMEND becoming comfortable with this idea of wholeness. It is not whole to deny you have any darkness in you, or to be afraid of owning it. If you visualise a figure 8 on its side, or an infinity symbol ∞, you can visualise yourself travelling around its shape. The right half can be your light side and the left half your dark side. They are of equal size and weight. As you let your energy flow along the path you will encounter obstacles slowing your movement.

The infinity symbol is a flowing meditation, if you find it difficult to imagine the movement with your mind, use your arm. Make the symbol as large as necessary. Your arm will show you the information you want it to. This is how dowsing works, the answer is already inside yourself, as when a water diviner picks up underground water vibrations through their feet. They then use their arm(s) to deliver the message through rods in a way that is clear to them. Take your arm and follow the symbol, asking to be shown where you have a blockage in your relationship with the light and the dark. Keep going, one side will be easier than the other and everyone is different in their life experiences and blocks. At this stage in your spiritual development many of you only need to be aware of the nature of the past experience that leads to a block, in order to release it permanently. Let them all go so you can become whole.

Be alone in a quiet, meditative state and start moving. *Ask us for help* in working with the symbol. You will travel to the first place you have a blockage, then ask yourself "What do I need to look at here?" There are pictures and words that we can use to start you thinking along the right lines. At the first stop you will be at the youngest point in your life, the second you will be older and so on. These memories will arise on the side of the light and the dark, as tears can arise from a loving experience or a miserable one. Memories contain energy and we are looking to heal these memories and blend the strength of their energy into a homogenous whole. The way becomes smoothed and the travelling easy and light. Around and around the infinity symbol, learning from your past with the perspective of an adult, healing old pain with the help of angels. Let the flow of energy heal them before moving ahead.

After a few days of travelling on your infinity symbol it will be running more smoothly. When the way is smooth, try to shrink the moving ∞ smaller until it is as small as a bow tie, a moving flow of energy. Then tug it smaller, smaller, smaller until it seems to be losing its definition. You are aiming to bring the two sides of the symbol into the centre where there is nothing except the smallest possible dot, one that can't be divided any further. Just keep asking us for help, and stating to yourself you are going to make it the smallest dot there is and hold it in your heart. That is the point of unity and wholeness where light and dark are one, if you look inside the dot there is nothing there except you. A long time ago the smallest possible dot began your universe, expanding outwards to become everything that is here now in the big bang. The universe is made of light and dark and choices.

When you start practicing with the smallest possible dot, while holding it in your heart you will hit the moment of balance. Then it may slip away needing a fresh effort to return to balance. Try and hold it for twenty seconds, that feeling of energy, balance, uprightness, peace. Now try it by running a method of healing energy, like Reiki, through yourself at the same time. Feel it become supported by the energy and you can hold it effortlessly as long as you are channelling energy. During your every day life you probably will not be in this balanced space unless you consciously place it in your heart again.

It can be done more quickly each time. Balance can be felt in your own person as a return to "normal", to a time when wholeness was once taken for granted. Life steps up a level when you are balanced, it allows you to make more of your time and opportunities because you are whole. Imagine how hard it is to do your best everyday with various parts of your soul incapacitated. Humanity is ready to live their lives in a balanced way again and some of you will do this exercise easily. Many people have worked towards living a balanced life for multiple lifetimes.

Everyone who practices this balanced healing on an unbalanced Earth helps the Earth. You are providing wholeness and balance, not just in your little human body but also in your energy fields. It's your energy fields that help settle the Earth's energy. When a group meets for Earth healing, the energy is enhanced, increasing exponentially so three become as nine, ten become as one hundred. One hundred balanced souls is a big help!

When you experience detrimental swings in climate the Earth is struggling, too. She is trying to rein in the imbalances and settle the climate again, this is where balanced help from humanity will help offset the damage done by other humans. We angels have been working with humanity to devise useful ways to help, this is a technique that can be done daily or in groups. Please try it.

If you think of those who profit from harming the Earth and others who counteract this damage, then the entire human race is on a large infinity symbol of light and dark. Just keep on your own journey of flowing around the infinity symbol, meditating and removing your blockages, acknowledging the dark while choosing actions of light. Those who despoil the Earth are far, far fewer than those who love her and look after her. Look around the entire world at the many farmers and people who daily live outside in her company and remember they help you balance the light.

17

Why Have Free Will?

WHEN A BEING has any sort of presence in this universe they are gifted with free will. Everything has free will, from the souls that never incarnate to the souls that live on planets. Angels have free will and we choose to honour our Creator and follow His wishes. When humanity designed this learning experience, this game of life, it chose rules that veiled many layers of existence. When you come to choose for yourself you have very little information on which to base your choices. This is actually the whole point of your game. Can you remember that you are a tiny part of God when you can't see what you are doing? Remembering relies almost completely on your acceptance that you have light and dark in your makeup and choosing to be whole.

Angels have no problem at all in being whole, whether we are working for the light or dark. We are not wearing blindfolds, not even the one that veils time, so we see how our actions affect absolutely everything from the first day of our existence. We could see the end of the universe when we stood at the beginning of time. When we made our choices we saw all the ramifications of that choice. It makes it easier for us to follow our pathway of light to see how each suggestion plays out in advance. Our universe is timeless, it ends when every being here has remembered who they are.

Humanity can puzzle over their choices for a long time before they make a move, and then they often simply hope it works out all right. We never have to do that, we can always see how it will work out. We own our wholeness as beings of two halves. When you look at another person and ask "how can they be so cruel?", it is their dark half acting. Their light half is blocked and they aren't using it very often. If you meet someone who says they have dealt with their shadow side and they are now only light, it's not true. They are still whole but could be afraid to acknowledge they have a dark side. They are either too afraid to look, or don't know how to deal with the darkness they find there. If you meditate on an infinity loop you will find the dark side of yourself is seldom very bad.

At first when you begin to notice and heal your fears surrounding the dark side of your soul, often you feel surprise at what is uncovered. Other people may have taught you that you must turn away from the dark and be only light. Often a person lives their life afraid of what they won't look at, afraid of being bad or evil and being punished one day. We, who are beings of light, understand why you have been taught this, that fear of the darkness affects student and teacher alike and it can seem too hard to look at what you fear. What do you think is inside you?

There are extreme examples of human cruelty leaving you wondering if they have been taken over by demons or are themselves just evil. Not everything is demonic possession, although that certainly happens. The real person is reduced to occupying a small corner of their own body. Don't get carried away with the idea that something must be the fault of demons and not human. This is where free will and choice come in, acknowledging humanity's capacity for darkness just as every being has a capacity for love. In the entire world how many mass murderers are you aware of, and how many people are not? There are about as many extremely evil people as there are extremely good people, the rest fall somewhere in the middle. Most people have a kindness and compassion that makes our hearts swell with emotion.

In the past there has been a tendency to blame others for anything that's gone wrong in their lives. This escalates to whole populations rising up against those they perceive as other than themselves, outside their tribe, race or religion. All darkness is seen as held in another person's soul giving one a duty of stamping it out. When someone owns their own dark half this feeling is reduced, they recognise they may have been the cause of their own problems. It is freeing to live this way with your eyes open to your own strengths and weaknesses. You begin to understand your life and see the greater picture of all humanity. With understanding comes compassion. With compassion comes oneness and ascension.

The object in creating this universe of polarity in shades of black, white and grey is to let people exercise their free will. Every human on this planet has free will and chooses for themselves. Being whole allows you to understand the difference between choosing good or evil. When all the choices have been made and the consequences have taken place the information is returned to the Creator. He breathed the universe out and one day will draw it back in.

Your soul is made up of light and dark characteristics, such as love and kindness, or impatience, envy, or laziness. Anything dark that scares you is you. When you stop, turn and look without fear at the dark - you will find an aspect of God that is not light, but is still part of Him. It is placed into your soul's make-up so that you will be like Him, a being of light and dark.

Angels of light choose not to behave in an evil manner, we do not try to bring souls to God through misery and despair. The dark angels have the sole purpose of doing exactly that - bringing souls to God through pain. We chose to work with joy, love and bliss. The important point is that everyone, in the final end, returns to God through light or dark pathways. When they recombine together as one they will have different tales to tell God about Himself and what He is like. He set the framework and we all participate within it by making our choices through free will. The Creator loves every part of His creation, He loves the dark side equally with the light. Love yourself, acknowledge your light and dark sides and become whole.

18
Moving Away From Global Markets

WHY WOULD WE describe a way to balance yourself and offer to help unless we thought is was very important for what is coming next on Earth? If you finished the previous chapter and dismissed our technique, we suggest that you at least try it before reading further because there is now going to be a jump in energy in our actual words. Some of you will read the words in this book and take more away from them than others, you will have the energy underlying the words working on you. If you have been using the infinity loop technique this will assist your absorption of the new energy. If you are in the process of working with the loop the energy will help you succeed. If you read straight past the loop and never tried it then you will still enjoy the words about what is coming soon, but the energy will be more of a trickle. We're not trying to pressure any one, but every book written has energy in its words. If you pick up the wrong kind of book (especially some occult books) there can be some very dark energies that affect you. We write our books on angel wings instead of paper, we only try to help people find the light. And, after all, using the loop to heal the memories that cause pain can only help. Painful memories have had some people in psychotherapy for years! It's definitely time to move forward now.

A wave of new Earth energy arrived in June 2018 with a jolt like electricity. It jump-started the Earth like those electric paddles restarting a heart after a heart attack. Earth was not dying, of course, but it helped her to change her rhythm. Who remained on their feet during the shift, the balanced people or the ones standing off-centre? Who carried on the next day taking everything in their stride with a smile on their face? There is pleasure in being ready for anything new, coping with life as it comes and proving to yourself how capable you are. We hope this was you!

Some people were knocked over by the jolt and when they tried to rise up on their feet found that they were standing on a planet that was rocking. Down they went again and this has been their life, trying to get upright ever since. Their experience has been one of life sliding away out of their control, a small, gentle avalanche started with all their ideas and possessions moving out of their grasp. They crawl after them and the avalanche moves everything away out of reach faster still. This experience does not lead to happiness for these people, nor do they understand what is happening. For the first time in their lives they can't manipulate their reality. They pay no attention to the Earth and missed all her signals about what is happening.

There are billions of people on the planet who are in touch with the Earth and have begun to alter their lives. At first they thought about what they were feeling, then they simply changed what they were doing because this rhythm doesn't require a lot of thought, it only asks for action. The change starts by shaking people with a lively rhythm, so the effect is similar to shaking someone awake. This wake-up call was heard by some and they changed their actions. This changing of people's actions is the whole point of altering the rhythm.

Recent examples of people changing their actions is present in the drive to remove the kinds of plastic packaging found most frequently in the oceans. There is love for the Earth among so many people who are suddenly thinking "No more single-use plastic products for me!" This has come about as people are informed and once they think about it, they are committed. They don't want to hurt their planetary home and they will use their purchasing power to ask for more multi-use and biodegradable items where they can. This is the division of half the planet walking in one direction to help the planet, while the other half walks the opposite way. Progress is difficult while this continues, but that will all change. The tipping point will come soon and helping the planet will start to include governments and corporations. In this case it is like a scale where many, many pebbles begin to outweigh the boulders on the other side. Your individual contribution is one of those important pebbles.

A level playing field can never be achieved while the scales are weighed down with boulders, but it is a mistake to think these corporations can just be removed by wishing it to be so. They fade as their customers turn and walk away. Again, it is the way to contribute a pebble to the scales by ceasing to be their customer. There were some quite large firms even ten years ago that are now gone as the market changed. There will be a change from the global market for goods to one centred on local goods and food supplies. Transporting goods does not help the planet; this is the kind of thought that will become most important to consumers as they shop. They won't want to play along with the corporations any more. They already don't want to harm the planet. Once they make the connections many will alter their actions.

19

Living in Darkness

THERE WAS A time, not very long ago, when fields and hedgerows were filled with the sounds of birds and insects and the oceans were full of fish. How long has it been since divers were able to find tropical coral reefs where there were many kinds of fish in great numbers? Twenty years? Thirty? Now the oceans need your help. If there are no fish swimming and maintaining the ocean's energy flow the energy becomes stagnant. Your oceans have always been great reservoirs of light surrounding each continent and island. The flow of the oceans help give the planet its light, they balance the slow moving energy of the land. When life is absent in the oceans it is a huge problem for Earth. It is a way to kill the planet by reducing flow and letting the oceans become lifeless marine deserts, stagnant and without light. More than any other part of your world the oceans need to be rescued, in order to save yourselves.

What happens if no one saves the oceans and they die through over-fishing, oil spills, chemical waste, pollution, plastic bottles, etc? Beautiful and devoid of life they surround the land, waves moving on the surface. Don't the waves count, and the deep ocean currents? We are looking for balance and are searching for the puzzle pieces that make up that balance. An empty ocean is filled with the consciousness of water, as is your kitchen sink. Life is everywhere, it just isn't always like a human or insect. Life is in water and stones, created by the One who gives life, they each exist to learn about themselves. Water in oceans and rivers learns about itself in partnership with other life, such as animals and vegetables that live in the sea. It is so important that all life has the opportunity to learn, that on your planet there is a deep despair over the way some species have been deprived of their lives. They are extinct now and missing from your balance, you have to exist in an unbalanced world and still manage to learn everything you came here to learn. The sadness of the planet every time it loses a species is acute while the species itself sadly moves on to a new planet and starts over. Bees are one of the more recent species to begin their exodus to another planet, crowded out of their living space. The excitement for these species to share a planet with humanity wore off a long time ago.

The willingness to kill other species instead of living alongside them is another way of expressing dark energy. The light that is found in love for all is often missing when it comes to pests and pestilences, among others. Even bacteria and viruses are a creation of God. Love can change the way you approach the problem of a cockroach infestation. How can you both live in balance without spoiling each other's lives? They have a right to live and so do you, find space for the others who share your world. Cockroaches are single-minded survivors, they hold that energy on the planet for everyone else.

This then, is about being whole and enabling your personal ascension. Balance and wholeness are siblings and they help each other exist. Partial people can never be wholly balanced unless they use healing techniques like the infinity loop for a few minutes a day. That way they help themselves and everyone else. True balance is approaching for the Earth as she readies to right herself on her axis. This will happen before twenty years has passed, until then everything that can be done to enhance balance will make the transition easier. The Earth being balanced will help humanity to balance.

In the past the Earth was not tipped over on her axis. She has spent the majority of her existence in an upright state. The change came when humanity began its learning experience by wearing a blindfold, hiding the higher dimensions. This sent your game wildly askew and your unbalanced behaviour became the dominant energy on Earth.

She couldn't stop herself from tipping over like a drunk with that energy raging on her surface. If you think this is an exaggeration, you are the only species that kills itself without any understanding of what that means. If two lions fight over a pride of females they know why they are doing it. Humanity has committed mass slaughter for false reasons, manipulated by a few who could see money to gain while others lost their lives. Lions kill each other as part of the rules of their game, the strongest male fathers the cubs. Humanity wanders lost in the dark.

Long ago at the beginning of the human game here on Earth you chose blindness for yourselves. We angels assisted you through our teachings and directed our help at keeping you moving forward and continuing your learning. You are still making progress in the same exact way: very, very slowly. Its the nature of your game. You have not run out of time yet to finish, but as the universe is changing around you, there are completed games on other planets that are preparing to pack up and go home. 'Home' being where they rejoin the Creator. This universe is in the pre-preliminary phase for its end and that is new, a 2018 development. It means no more new games and those games that are wandering around in circles will have to find a way to complete and move ahead. What difference does this make to what's happening on Earth? It makes a difference to the human soul, where you all meet and make decisions. Do you want to hold other planets back? Do you want to miss your target and fail in your chosen game? Do you want to return to the Creator through the pathways of misery or happiness? Humanity has chosen and knows it will have to substitute new rules, rules that are designed to be dropped into a game running somewhere near its end. How close are all of you to finishing? Ninety-seven percent done, now. In our book *Stepping Through the Looking Glass* you were ninety-eight percent complete, so you are backing away from oneness at the moment.

The human soul is aware of this backward step and it is substituting tiny variations in the rules of life almost daily. You are not changing the main points of the contract with Earth, but are finding ways to meet your targets. As long as you allow the awakening of humanity to unfold naturally, you are staying true to your original plan. Right now you are walking backwards slowly and making the same mistakes you've made in the past. This is okay up to a point, but you are where there is little further use in this and only walking forward will help you reach ascension.

When we say walking backwards, we mean every step that increases the distance between you and anyone else. It's time to stop seeing the differences in other people and see instead all the characteristics you have in common, to stop seeing them as "other". When you see them as a mirror image of yourself you are almost there, learning to see yourself looking back from the eyes of other people. That will be nearing the end of the pathway to personal ascension, leaving only the joy of discovering yourself in all of God's creations. When your happiness increases you know you're on the right track.

It's been a difficult journey for humanity, one of the hardest ever devised, it has strengthened you and formed you into warriors.

20

The Earth's Mega-Soul

THE RULES OF your game never really provided a level playing field, you did not have enough information or insight. By being blind to nine dimensions and seeing only height, width and depth, humanity struggled to find any direction in which to move and too often appeared like a swarm of ants. We did all we could to help, and the dark angels did all they could to mislead you. Contrast this with the animal species who set up their rules for a game in all the dimensions. They had adjustments to make through contact with other species who often saw them as prey, this contact helped them grow and multiplied their experiences. Ecosystems were formed where interacting species were in balance with the variables of weather and natural disasters. Humanity had a role to play here and at times fitted into wider planetary life. Part of the enduring fascination with the Native American culture was how they fit in and played their part. When there are discussions about recreating original groups of animals in Yellowstone Park, they have been leaving out the top predator, man. A level playing field can be a system or ecosystem that allows every being a chance to live the best life they can.

A level playing field also refers to every being having the chance to live the life they planned for on the Earth. All species arrived with a contract, a goal and a game plan. Their goal was always to reach group ascension if they could before finishing their contract with the Earth. Every species that worked together has now accomplished this, they are only remaining on Earth to see if humanity can make the leap to this higher level of understanding.

Humanity began their time here by working with all other life forms, then many people became greedy. It was as if the goal had changed from ascension to seeing who could accumulate the most riches before dying. To forget why you came to a planet is rare, as it is the inmost driving force for any being. One of the few traces of it remaining in humans is when someone says "There must be more to life than this!" You are here to remember, but you have taken many steps backwards on the way to understanding. Humanity was much further along a few centuries ago, learning and walking steadily on an upward path until they slid back down again. There are some things to relearn before reaching the same point again. One of them is to love you neighbour as yourself, including the non-human ones. Humanity has travelled a long, long way on this path devised to teach themselves who they are. The information is all available and it only takes a few more small steps to put the pieces together and understand it in your hearts, then act based on your knowledge. By doing so you will be one of the first to ascend as an individual, while helping to lead the way for your whole soul group. The process of ascension has begun slowly, but at least some people are moving towards those considered "other". As we see it, that is moving towards the finishing line in your game on Earth.

When this game finishes and humanity ascends - what happens next? What does it mean for you?

This universe is set up as a contained space to experience life, it's flexible like a balloon. When you blow up a balloon there is only one entrance for the air and in a similar way the universe expanded from a single point. However, there are all kinds of side entrances built into the universe, for example there are portals that open when it is necessary to leave one universe and enter another. The Archangel Melchizadek is another, acting as a bridge to the Creator with his feet outside the universe and his head inside. Another word for this bridge is the Christ and Melchizadek is the angelic Christ. The

Creator is in the centre of countless universes of His own making and He is completely aware of what is happening in each, because of the Christs. He dispersed himself out into these universes, and one day He will draw them back in to become one in a great in-breath. He learns who He is by each being learning who they really are.

When humanity finishes its time on Earth the greater human soul will have reunited and become one, and it will be a huge relief to become whole again for all the individual human beings. It's going to be a bit like waking from a long sleep with many, many interesting dreams. The dreams are not real, being awake and conscious is reality. This single soul, now wiser than ever, will choose what to do next. If humanity has ascended into light they can complete their contract with Earth by joining her in a mega-soul of light. If they do not ascend they will have exhausted their opportunities to try again. We would be sorry to see this because we know how close you have come to ascension. Earth's original plan to collect together all these souls and combine with them into one soul of brightest light is a key moment in the history of the universe. The light of this mega-soul tips the universe's balance towards the light. Earth is the planet where light and dark are balanced on a knife edge, what happens here has a greater effect because there are few planets left who have not settled for light or dark at this time. This tip towards the light will start the process of return. Your inclusion as a wise ascended soul brings a warrior quality to the group, humanity has fought hard on Earth to be included and rise to ascension. Joining the mega-soul and returning to the Creator in light has been a long held goal of humanity, you and Earth planned for this together and she's waiting for you. However, you still have a choice not to ascend.

When we wrote that humanity has already ascended on other planets, these were steps leading to this planet and this experience. Humanity's time on Earth was planned to be the final game, and it was looking forward to the day it joined with the other Earthly souls. It would be a step closer to rejoining the Creator in wholeness. Humanity is a splinter itself of the Creator and, by rejoining with all the Earthly species it will bask in the comfort of the greater connection. Will there be even larger challenges as a member of this mega-soul group? That's the nature of the universe, but you will not face the challenges alone.

What does it mean for you to be a splinter of a splinter? We feel we can say with confidence that we have never seen anything as heartbreakingly lonely as humanity in this game. You have loneliness built in to your time here as a significant challenge and you have learned about it thoroughly. You're not even aware that there is another way to live. We see how much the loneliness has reduced the love and comfort for you in these many lives. No wonder you find it so hard. You may think that visiting and talking with friends relieves loneliness, but that just scratches the surface. Your thoughts are so private by design you are able to disguise yourself with any number of masks. You protect yourselves so no one really knows what you feel and what you are thinking; you fear they'll despise you. In most other species they share all these thoughts and the effort of holding up a mask is never needed. Knowledge and familiarity increase their love for each other. Beings are not afraid of being so bad they are unlovable, love increases as they see their common traits. Your masks keep up barriers that also keep out love, and fear increases the darkness of your lives here. There is nothing more important in life, nothing that feeds and strengthens the soul as love.

Human society is going through a backwards phase of hate, where the amount of hatred and darkness is in the ascent. We write that human ascension includes taking action and that it's not enough to know in your hearts that you are all one. Mass hatred is anti-ascension in energy and we challenge you to find actions that lead towards love and light. Get accustomed to holding a current thought or idea with love and see if it blends with love or jars against it. Prepare to make changes in everything you do to combat this infection of hatred. If the hate grows there will be more division and violence, if love grows it will fade away and people will unite to work together again. There are many, many of you that fill your hearts with love and you need to lead the way toward the light. This is your role in this lifetime as long as hatred and division last. There are so many different ways to act, as many as there are people in the world. What talent and skill can you bring to the aid of your soul group?

Part Three
Road to the Top

21

The Role of the New Mega-Soul

WHERE DOES humanity go from here? Divisiveness is on the increase and threats are intensifying against anyone considered different from oneself. Some wonder how everything got like this, and when life will go back to the way it was? In the greater scheme of life in the universe, is this what is supposed to be happening right now on Earth? Is it a necessary part of the plan for ascension? Is humanity failing?

As long as you have not yet ascended, you can still fail to ascend, but the game isn't over yet. The recent divisive energy is affecting human lives. When there is a quality of energy like this, and if you "go with the flow" you will be deeply affected by it's negativity. If you work against it and love your neighbour as yourself, it will have a smaller negative effect on you. The energy of division is meant to make it easier at this time to identify those whose time on Earth is over. It shakes things up. There are those whose actions lead the way in separating people into smaller groups and falling from love into hatred for their fellow humans. Do you think the greater human soul hasn't noticed this? When it makes plans for the best chance for ascension it sees these people as those whose time is up. Not valueless, not wrong, as every experience has value, but they've run out of time on Earth. They are the slow learners at a time when everything is speeding up. Others have learned the lessons of oneness in earlier incarnations. Religion also plays a role in dividing one from another and increasing dislike and distrust. Politics relies on dividing one set of the voters from the other, often by any means possible, to build a core group to maintain their power.

You could think of this energy as acting like a large sieve. When you sift flour in the kitchen you get smooth flour in a bowl and anything else is kept in the sieve and discarded. The division is made by the fine wires of the sieve. That is what this energy does by separating people so they fall around the wires and end up in a bowl, smooth and homogenous, while others are discarded. The energy acts like the ribs of a fan being opened out and the divisions grow wider and wider. You are pushed farther and farther apart until the sieving is finished. Those who are not homogenized in the bowl have no further place on Earth. There is no one left to hide behind when they find themselves alone in the sieve. This energy will end and the sieving will be complete. Those in the sieve are exposed so they can be discarded either now or when they die.

This divisive energy wave has its origins closer to the Earth than some. As a local wave it flows from the Sun to the Earth. The Earth and Sun are in constant communication and energy waves of different vibrations can be arranged when necessary. The Sun does this for all the solar system, it uses its strength as a star to create waves and propel them outward. This particular wave started building in 2014 and continues into 2019. When the divisive energy is gone people will change their behaviour if they are followers, but the leaders may take a long time to realise the energy has shifted. Enacting plans made possible by one energy when there is a new energy in place is very difficult; it's like trying to drive a car that's out of fuel. The plan will be there but it will be very hard to move it forward. Opposition will grow.

This sifting is important, it is why humanity had to take these steps backwards; to expose what's been hidden in your societies, to bring it to the surface where it could be seen. As we keep reminding you, most people are good and kind and would have to be deceived into following hateful paths. Those who lead movements of hate do not fall into the good and kind category. You will see quite a variety of leaders with their true natures exposed, far more cruel and greedy than the people who support them. They'll have no where to hide.

Why would the Earth ask for exactly this kind of help? It seems a bit risky to create sometimes violent divisions on her surface. Divisions and violence - all experiences are useful and valued. When rebuilding a society it can be shaped differently than it was before, leading you into a new experience. Humanity was stuck in a pattern of behaviour that was useless for reaching ascension. If you ever wondered "how are we going to ascend when we are so divided?" - you weren't. You all have to be one together to ascend. There have been moments in the past when it looked like people and nations would join together in a spirit of co-existence for their mutual benefit. As you headed into a position of opposition the Earth asked for help. She is still waiting for you to ascend right up to the point when she can't wait any longer. What has been a long, long game is finally reaching its conclusion, one way or the other.

The Earth is on a journey of her own. She's had a number of previous incarnations hosting species that ascended and moved on. What is different this time is that this is her last time at this level of existence. She made an extreme plan with humanity and took a chance on helping you to pull it off. She was strong in the light and as experienced as any of her sister planets. She had the extra benefit of having the first species to work with her stay here as a twin soul; the crystals that ascended with her, remain today to help out of love. (The story of the crystals and the Earth are in *Planet Earth Today*). This planet will have many unusual stories to tell the Creator Who Loves Us All one day. Humanity's time here was so challenging and costly to her in many ways that she is ready for her next phase. The challenges that she has overcome have resulted in her own accelerated growth and she's ready to move forward.

The next step for her is the giant mega-soul. This soul is intended to be made up of all the species on the planet. When these species become one they share their lives and themselves. When you see animals eating one another on Earth that is part of who they are. Many species are meeting in this mega-soul for the first time, such as a lizard and a polar bear. They are buzzing with the intensity of everyone else's experiences. "What was your life like?" As they discover lives lived in deserts or in the Arctic, new information is shared and becomes part of their understanding and a part of their new story. First they joined together and now they are discovering who they have become. As one consciousness they learn about themselves through their past experience as individual souls. There will come a point when they have completely blended and stop asking questions, looking outwards they will wonder about the stories of those in the universe who have not yet united with them.

This is therefore a tiny part of the Creator and the process that He planned as a way to learn about Himself. He will listen to everyone's stories and know that they are about Him in the same way as the stories of the mega-soul are about its members. The audacious plan the Earth made was to take a step into her future to the time when she will become one with the Creator and everything He created at the end of the universe.

If humanity does not ascend with the Earth it will continue to exist in a lonely state, which will now look quite lonely in comparison to the companionship inside the mega-soul. It will miss out on the bliss, it will miss assisting the mega-soul in its next plan.

The mega-soul was planned to unite ascended species and anchor that light in a soul so large and bright that it would influence any section of the galaxy or universe it visited. It would tip the balance towards the light of even the darkest stars and planets. Some of these bodies have been sitting in stagnant energy for eons now and it's time for them to change and move. They will find it hard to begin the process, but they can be helped to flow by a soul this large and bright. You may think the universe is always adversarial and the dark and the light will automatically battle, however light and dark angels are pragmatic beings, each looking to bring information back to the Creator. If challenging the status quo and shaking things up will be of the greatest benefit, then that will be their first choice of action. If you imagine a very dark world and stagnant society, introducing light changes everything. Where there was only darkness, now there is a pinprick of light and all eyes are drawn to it. That's enough to initiate change. The shift from dark to light is another tale to save up and tell the Creator.

The Earth's mega-soul will behave as a normal soul in the universe except it will never again be a physical planet hosting experiences. It will take on its new role of anchoring light and living in a higher energy state. No longer will it reside in your solar system two-thirds of the way out on an arm of the Milky Way galaxy, it will be fluid and free to move where it can help the most. This will be a very wise soul filled with the combined experiences of many and will be how the Earth lives in ascension with it's guests.

Humanity's goal was always to join this mega-soul. Not every ascension follows this pattern, but all ascensions will lead to learning at a higher level and all involve accruing more and more information to tell the Creator about Himself. The challenges that arise will not be the challenges of a physical planet, but they will be new ones to suit the new level. The mega-soul itself will not be divided into smaller species again, it will remain as one new being. It will be the leading edge of light in the galaxy. From the very beginning humanity wanted to be a part of this.

22

Walk Yourself Into Ascension

B Y NOW YOU may wonder what else there is to learn before ascension, and how did you not learn it already? Earth has been humanity's home for a long time now and there has been more than one false start. Every time humanity was temporarily absent from the planet the human soul was busy working out a slightly new angle to fulfil the contract, then return for another try. You have learned many wonderful and hard lessons and now your goal is to practice living homogenously. Living in a blended, cohesive way like flour after it's been sieved into a bowl. You will need to live like you are all the same and no one is better or different from each other. You may think this will never happen, but from our point of view you are very close now. People are tired of living in toxic societies where inequality between the sexes, different skin colours, or different cultures are all reasons to be treated as lesser beings. Your own path is to do the best you can in every instance and contribute to the changes that are boiling under the surface of your societies.

The false starts in humanity's past have led to a great deal of wandering about and getting stuck in dead ends. Think of a maze and how one reaches the centre only through trial and error. Humanity has covered every step of the maze, some of those steps twice, and now stands with one foot lifted to take the final step. You hesitate there at the opening to the centre not sure if you are ready to firmly step forward onto the ground. You look around and there are people behind you, lost and hoping you know the way. Stepping into the centre you achieve personal ascension by releasing everything that keeps you from loving every living being on Earth. You see yourself as one with God and everything He has created. Your oneness takes in every part of the universe, going far beyond your life here. You look through His eyes as He looks out on the universe He created and it fills your heart with love and awe. Any time you wish you can return to His point of view again, never forgetting what you really are.

Meanwhile the people walking behind you through the maze notice that you live your life in a way they wish to emulate. They follow in your footsteps and, because you went first and showed them the path, they have an easier journey and soon join you in the centre. The whole process of ascension speeds up and more and more people live and love in such a way that their example leads others to self-realisation. Human ascension will occur ever more swiftly as one person after another remembers they are a part of God, and that God loves all His creations. The vibration of the entire human soul rises with each individual ascension. It will happen because of the actions you take in the lifetime you are living now. You can only ascend for yourself, but you can help by showing others the way. Everyone is aware subconsciously of their drive to ascend and has the ability to recognise the road when they see it. They just haven't see it yet. There are some people alive now who can only see money, status and power, even these people have the same inner drive to ascend. It lies buried at the bottom of everything else that occupies their minds while their hearts are neglected. Money is the most effective way to distract yourself and pulls you away from everything that matters. The second is your mobile phone.

The road to ascension then is made up of almost eight billion roads for those living on Earth now, and many billions more for those not currently in physical bodies. Some of those people have finished incarnating now, those who have ascended and those others whose actions do more harm than good. Humanity became wildly enthusiastic about splintering its soul on this planet into ever larger numbers of people but there wasn't enough energy to maintain a strong spirit in each of these bodies. Sometimes you hear about someone being an old soul, they tend to stand out because they have more depth. They used their lives well to learn when an opportunity presented itself. Depth of experience leads to ascension.

What about those people who strike you as shallow, without depth? They could be here simply to show you an aspect of humanity that also requires your love, another side of yourself.

There are quite a few incarnations remaining for many of you, which sounds like humanity will be here for a long time yet to come. This brief time remaining at the end of your long stay here will involve quick turn-arounds between lives. This rapidity is to place on Earth those who have consciously awakened, bringing that knowledge and awareness through to help. This is seen to be the best plan now and is why we have previously written that the babies born since 2012 are so very special. Many who reached personal ascension will choose to return to assist those cleaning and repairing the planet.

Ascension removes barriers between yourself and the rest of the universe. Even when ascended masters return to Earth with a partial blindfold, they will receive information through their interconnectedness with all things. An ascended master is still a human being and needs everyone else to reach the same level before the soul ascends. These are very exciting times for humanity and for those of us that watch and help you! For the Earth and the rest of the universe it will be so short a time, it is as if you will be finished and ascended in the next hour. To us it feels like humanity is ready, we just need more of you to take the final step and alter your everyday actions. Looking at everyone with love in your eyes changes both you and them and spreads outwards like ripples in a pond. Try it, all are strangers to you on Earth, even your closest family members. Walk yourself into ascension step by step.

One role of the ascended masters is to care for the Earth by maintaining an energy grid around the planet. In this they act as one with other species such as animal and insect ascended masters with a few human masters mixed in. The other species ascended a level with the Earth in 2015 and at that time assumed responsibility for maintaining the energy grid. The Earth is supported by the grid which acts as a framework for the new mega-soul. It's like an energy skeleton and gives life a blueprint for the next phase. With this many souls joined together into one, the energy in the grid is immense. They help steady the Earth in her present physical incarnation while she helps humanity complete its game. Every species in the grid looks at humans and sees them as part of itself.

On Earth it is possible to link to the energy grid when you are low energetically or need some additional help with healing. This is a good connection for all Earth healing groups to use to enhance the amount of energy coming in for the group. To link, simply say "I now link to the energy grid around the planet." As the grid is held by those who are ascended in love it is this energy that you connect to and it cannot be used for harm. This is also good for private healing projects where you may not be able to gather a group together each time. The grid can be your healing group.

The energy grid's main purpose at this time is stabilisation of the planet. When the grid intercepts solar flares it increases in strength, holding the Earth stable. This grid also grows stronger daily as more energy pours into it from the Sun. Scientists are aware of a number of different energetic frequencies flowing out from the Sun and the extremely high vibrational waves are destined for the energy grid while other, lower frequencies serve different purposes for the Earth. When the Earth has stability problems, as she does now from climate change, she is held in love by this grid, steadying her. The Earth doesn't want to be wobbling out of control at this time of major change and you can help her balance through Earth healing groups. If the Earth didn't need help right now, ascended masters holding the grid could allow a more flowing energy grid to exist, less rigid and allowing smoother change. This wobble and the firm grip of the grid contribute to a rocky ride for Earth and her inhabitants.

Earth had made her plans for this time of her soul's evolution. She would look after all the life forms on her surface by providing them with everything they needed to live and learn about themselves. Earth created the most beautiful, paradise planet in the galaxy, where whatever the body needed it would find ready to hand. Animals spread from the tropics to the Arctic and humans followed in their footsteps, not completely separate but as part of a vast web of life. You were one of the top predators, and your role was echoed by big hunting cats, wolf packs, sharks, etc. Now you are the top predator, but you don't see the web or your place in it anymore. This was an unexpected development and is partly due to the length of time you have been on Earth. You deliberately chose to make your learning experience as hard as possible and that has allowed a great number of dead ends that wasted time to develop. It's been interesting for us to watch.

Among the dead ends are customs, religions, tribalism and so forth. They were not necessary to learn who you are, so humanity has wandered down any number of these pathways, learned a great deal and made their way back. They have not always learned to love one another or know who they really are. We can't imagine how many more of these dead ends you might create for yourselves if you had endless time on Earth, but it's time for the wandering to come to an end. In the years remaining on this planet for humanity you will begin to restrict the options and force yourselves onto a direct path. It may seem like there is too much happening at once: flooding, volcanoes, earthquakes, hurricanes, stock market crashes and social unrest. Each event removes options and forces everyone to look more closely at reality. There have been a great many lies told by all kinds of people until it is impossible to know what to believe. However the truth is there behind layers of black filth and these many events will help to expose it. So we urge you to detach yourselves from emotional adherence to lies and watch with balanced judgement. Remember what you see and look for cause and effect. Trust the core of light that is your human soul.

This sounds like humanity could ascend by crashing over the finishing line in a heap. It won't happen quite like that. As people are put into a position where they remember who they are, they will reach out a helping hand to strangers. Some people will be homeless because of where they live, such as low lying countries; they may have chosen that in this life deliberately to give others a chance to help when the time comes. While the Earth creates large events people will have the chance to help on a smaller, human level. This won't be one person saving millions, it will be millions of people saving others one by one. In the end you will gather and walk across the finishing line together.

23

Upsetting the Game Board

AS THE WAVE of divisiveness diminishes on Earth, people will wonder why they were so afraid of others.. As fear lessens there will be a return to peace. Everyone knows inside themselves that they are here to remember they are all one and every time their lives align with this inner knowledge they relax and become happier. Peace is necessary for this realisation to manifest; when there is strife and tension people concentrate on survival and put aside everything else. There has been very little peace on Earth in recent centuries.

A continuing stream of energy waves has been bathing the Earth in recent years. Energy waves of one sort or another are designed to achieve an outcome, they are to coax you into being happy. They strip away obstacles and make it easier for you to see yourself and remember that you're a loveable person, capable of loving and being loved. If you bobbed around in an ocean wave long enough you would be scrubbed clean and no longer be holding armfuls of useless possessions. Clean and energised you would be able to walk onto shore and choose the direction of your next steps and your next ideas. Be careful what you choose to pick up and carry, ideologies of hatred can be very heavy burdens, heavy enough to sink you down to your knees in the sand and be unable to move.

Energy changes always come first, they are then followed by physical changes. Waves of energy eventually work through the dense physical bodies of people, animals and trees. If you upset a chess board you would have to set all the pieces up again, hoping to remember where they were before. Waves are intended to upset game boards and the pieces will attempt to scramble to their feet.

Some are full of energy, some have no access to energy and won't rise again. This leaves spaces open that may have been squatted on for generations. There will be changes ahead.

Reading this you may wonder "what about me?" We can't talk to each of you individually and this guidance is for all. When changes begin to happen, you each need to leave behind ideas that are limiting. If you see an opportunity for yourself opening up then we urge you to step right in and take it. It could have belonged to someone in the past who is not there now. They may be moving sideways themselves and leaving a space free. In particular for those groups of people who have been blocked from opportunities this message is important. No one needs old baggage and beliefs holding them back and negative ideas have no more place in your lives. Empty spaces are new opportunities, livelihoods, relationships, etc. Leave fear of failure behind and go for it! The only thing that really matters is learning more about what you are capable of.

Earth is anticipating a period of chaos, a short topsy-turvy time of rebalancing. The top and bottom become jumbled together for a while and everyone will have an equal opportunity to have enough to enjoy their lives. The word "enough" is one of our favourites, where everyone has enough for their needs. You still have enough resources on this planet for almost eight billion people to live comfortably without hunger or worry, but the Earth's gifts simply haven't been shared out fairly. We never mean to imply that everyone will have exactly the same quantity of everything, but that the top and the bottom exist closer together socially and economically. Worry and fear are very dark energies for families and if you don't alleviate them the whole world increases in darkness. It won't matter whether your home is behind a security gate or not. Energy is not held back by gates.

Economic and social inequality are not naturally human in that you're not born as a baby with these qualities. They are learned and artificial. When something huge and life controlling is artificial like this, it has to be energetically maintained with a great deal of effort. A lot of energy goes into holding it in place. All of you on Earth contribute to providing this energy to maintain the illusion of inequality. If you think that only the wealthy put their energy into keeping an artificial society in place, then you need to understand there are simply not enough of them. They need you to keep them in their mansions. This means that each of you can choose to withdraw your support for an artificial society. How?

Turn away and find where you can still see the natural Earth. Behind you is a flickering screen of illusion created by man and filled with everything you are accustomed to in life. Some parts of the illusion are genuine, such as acts of kindness and loving human interactions. That is what every baby brings into the world when it is born. Every picnic and walk under the trees reminds you that there is an underlying, clean vibration of love. Trees are among the life forms that broadcast love. Even in treeless areas the natural Earth broadcasts the vibration of love. We suggest you familiarise yourself with what these vibrations feel like, their softness and warmth. When you return to your homes and jobs you will need to locate these vibrations and bring them to the forefront of your lives. Use the vibration of love as a roadmap. This is not an expensive task, it isn't boring or time consuming, it's food for the soul. It's lifting a veil and allowing you to balance, so every other part of your life works. From a point of wholeness and balance you will make different choices. Take your children outside with you and follow their lead.

Earthly societies have been structured in the pyramid shape for the last few thousand years, where money is concentrated at the top and the poorest make up the largest section at the base. It wasn't always like that and you are living through its demise now. It probably doesn't feel like the end to anyone yet, but that pyramid has grown to an impossibly pointy height, with the global billionaires at the top of a tall needle and everyone else a long way down. It looks like a square of wood with a nail hammered up through the middle, except this wood is trembling and dissolving. The energy is not there to hold the nail upright any longer, it is only supported by the lack of understanding that it can all be let go. It could be released away in a matter of weeks if everyone worked together. That's the quickest way to get back to everyone having enough.

The stock markets are a series of binary figures inside of computers and if the numbers fall they not closely linked to the real value of the companies. Real money is based on real things like sales, labour and buildings on the land. You can touch reality and it has value. Perhaps you are investors in the stock market? There is still a role for it as a place where businesses can raise money for expansion by selling shares of ownership. This is barely the function of the markets now. The wealthy have to do something with the money they've accumulated and a lot of it is parked in shares.

Topsy-turvy doesn't mean people have to hurt each other or fight over resources. There has always been enough on Earth for everyone. It is a change in attitude and focus, a change in people's willingness to continue playing by rules that only benefit a few. It's walking away in a different direction using gifts that were previously stifled. It will be a relief as it's no fun playing a game that's been rigged against you, one that you can never win. Times are changing.

24

How Do You Change the World?

WHAT CAN YOU expect to happen? How can change affect your lives? You were living outdoor lives associated with food production for millennia. Fishing, herding animals, growing crops and transporting them to market. Suddenly this was no longer the case and a few people were able to grow enough to feed many more and much of this was due to better transport. There was more time to make other products and create new industries leading to radically changing lives. Health has declined with pollution and life spans today are slowly edging downwards. At the same time people have developed wider interests and gained greater knowledge and they now have more time to think about spiritual matters. We approve of this change, you all deserve to have lives that are interesting and enjoyable. When you spend all your time finding shelter and food to feed yourselves, you have no time for anything more than survival. So many on Earth are simply trying to survive they have no leisure to remember why they are here.

We feel that there have been many, many times in the past when societies were balanced, interesting and enjoyable in their own way. The contents of societies would be mixed up in different combinations to create this balance and learn new lessons. One of the simplest is hunter-gatherer: they are happy when they find food easily and the seasons are kind to them. They don't need what you need to be as happy as you are.

Today you have an interesting mix of electronic entertainments, from movies and TV to the internet channels. There's lots for everyone to find and watch. Do you consider this as a period when humans are living enjoyable and healthy lives? There is a lot of underlying sadness in young people in their daily lives. This is crucial as the older generations die and pass their money down to a few wealthy offspring. These heirs will be living in a world that does not feel like the world of their parents, where there was greater wage equality; they will be living in a world made of impoverished and often hopeless wage-slaves. Energetically it is shaping up to be a dismal world, one that leads to the pathway of despair to find your Creator. It looks like a world designed by demons. In your Christian Bible you say "The love of money is the root of all evil", in other words, greed.

Greed is probably the single largest motivator for the activities of the wealthy and it's one of the largest background energies on Earth right now. Your lives are lived with this dark energy surrounding you. If you are aware of greed and the way it affects your world, can you walk away from its presence in your lives or are you always wanting more? You who have comparatively very little, could you embody something of real value? By real value we mean all those energies that make you blaze up with light like kindness and love, happiness, gratitude, truthfulness, honesty and integrity. These are only some of the qualities of light, qualities that will change the energy in your immediate area and far beyond. How do you change the world? By changing yourself.

If you value kindness more than money or possessions, what actions would be a regular part of your life? Everyone's at a different stage in their development so we are not going to make any rules here, we don't think you need them. When we talk about actions to go with your spiritual understanding we mean everything from healing groups to active philanthropy, there is something for everyone to do. And guess what? You came here to do everything you could to remember you are all one by interacting with each other. Material possessions never were part of the plan, except for those who knew that with great wealth comes great responsibility. These people are playing a high risk game with a greater chance of missing their goals. We see only a very few wealthy individuals on track to finish their lives achieving what they came in to learn.

Are we saying that you should shun a gift of money or a promotion and salary increase at work? No. We are saying that everyone needs to understand the world as it is today so you can negotiate obstacles and end by having learned the lessons you came in to learn. We may even help to smooth the path towards success for some so they can learn the harder lessons that wealth brings. If you won the lottery tomorrow what would you do with the money? What a challenge that could be!

We are pleased to say that there are many who are living the lives they incarnated to live. Young and old there is a sense of urgency to align with your life plans, a sense that you're not here to waste your lives and every moment can be directed towards the successful completion of your design. This is living the easy way, with the sense of fulfilment and peace that achieving your goals brings. It frees you from worry or caring so much about what others are getting up to. You are all on different paths to the same goal, you go your way and let others go theirs. When you feel like you are on the right path then you can comfortably extend a helping hand to others. These are the people who walk with their eyes fixed on the finishing line to ascension.

Now you may be wondering if you are anywhere near to walking on your chosen path for this life. We suggest taking the time to meditate in your daily lives, it is the most useful tool you have for clarity. It allows your brain to reach a level of relaxation difficult to reach in any other way and in this window of clarity you can make sensible choices. Every day is a series of choices and with a clear mind you will choose the ones that align with your purpose. Meditation allows you to hear your inner, wise self to guide you past obstacles. Some of you may even hear our voices when meditating. Angels tend to say something like what a great job you're doing, or

how proud we are of you. Listen for the love in our voices to know
we are there.

25

Truth

THERE WAS A time when only priests claimed to know what happened after death. As no one else seemed to know for sure what was coming they placed their trust in the authority of the priests. These belief systems were comforting and unifying where there was only one religion present in a nation or society. They formed the major religions that you are familiar with today. If a person doubted any part of their national religion they tended to keep their thoughts to themselves. It took a major prophet, fearless and dedicated to the truth as he saw it, to begin preaching a variation on his religion. Often these prophets introduced corrections and a relaxation of fear. They were interpreting what they perceived as truth and were doing their best to tell others. Today the major religions have splintered into many sects that interpret differently the words of their founding prophet.

This gives you a vast choice of interpretations of truth, an absolute tangle of pathways to find God by following the rules set out by a church leader you trust. In this book we are giving you the truth as we see it. How can you find your way through all these different versions of truth, including ours? We would like to give you some exercises in training your truth sensors. If in the end you believe what you feel is true, we could ask for nothing more.

Truth is crucial for reaching ascension, for you and for all of humanity. It's not a pleasant, optional extra on your life's journey. It's armour to protect you from the darkness, from becoming lost on your way. Lies are like the illusion of a roadblock with signs pointing to the left or right and tricking you into believing the way ahead is blocked. Lies trick you into taking actions you would never normally take, trick you into walking away from your path. At the end of your life you are lost, once again, and weep to find you failed to learn and achieve those lessons you meant to learn. Lies are the most successful tool of the dark angels to prevent joy and happiness, to prevent living in bliss and reaching ascension. If you can detect the difference in vibration between true and false you will find your life changed. You are human, and human beings are strong in the light.

Truth is a vibration of light and love, and lies are a tool of darkness. How can we state that with such assurance? We look at the end results and we also look back at the time before the lie was spread. We can see light and dark energy, a skill that is worth developing for yourself. We are presenting you with a mental exercise, training your mind to be strong when faced with someone telling you something you know is false. This happens continually in your countries, you are bombarded with lies. We go so far as to say that lying is expected and everything is "spun" or presented with only a tiny bit of truth among the lies. You need to turn away from these words and remember what you saw taking place for yourself at the time. Remember the experiences of yourself and your family and friends and what you saw with your own eyes. Remembering is paying attention and exercising your brain

Taking an example current today is the denial of the horror of the Holocaust, well documented at the time with photos and personal testimonies of prisoners and the eyewitness accounts of the soldiers who liberated the death camps. Now some say it never happened only because they see a gain for themselves in telling lies. You need to look at someone who is telling you that black is white and white is black and ask yourself, what have they got to gain?

Why aren't we telling you to go with your gut feeling or follow your heart? That comes later. You actually need a period of standing back from lies and not get caught up in the emotion of what you are hearing. Liars know that they can gather more people more quickly when they raise the emotions, especially in a crowd. Some people go to a rally just to have these emotions raised, there is a fun element to participating in something with everyone else. "Everyone" being people who all feel alike. Only someone who's present through listening and not feeling can sift through the rhetoric to hear the words of truth. Watching with their eyes they can make memories that are true. It requires practice to stand back.

When you have created clear memories, unclouded by emotions, you can compare what you heard with what actually happened. There is a lot of double-speak now where if something takes place the exact opposite will be claimed. Today you have to really work to remember what was happening in the recent past. Constructing a series of events that you are pretty sure are true will train you in spotting cause and effect, truth and lies. Many times an action leads to a new chain of events, very often with citizens losing an established right because of a perceived new emergency. Here you have to be so careful to observe events at the time and remember what was happening just before, or possibly years earlier.

It's not easy to observe in a neutral fashion when emotions are deliberately being manipulated and heightened. Often it happens that you detect lies easiest when you disagree with someone, but even there you have stumbling blocks because not everything is always untrue. Certainly in politics you are being bombarded with so many lies from every direction that it seems impossible to be clear except for one thing - you can detect pathways of light, sparks of light, people of light (there are incarnate angels even in politics) a matching of the light of words and ideas to the light in your soul. You have a soul of light and it either matches your own high vibration or it clashes. This is far easier than it sounds.

26

It Doesn't Feel Right

SPEND AN HOUR on social media and read the mix of terrible stories about every political leader. Can one person truly be as black as they are painted? Some are, and you can tell by the dead body count as they rule their countries. The stories about other leaders have an element of truth surrounded by lies. How do you feel after your hour online reading these stories? Who gains from your sadness?

In our first book *Planet Earth Today* we wrote about the role of angels and demons in this universe and how it was designed as way for every being to experience polarity. Demons are dark angels with the job of bringing despair and misery into lives and when you read news stories that make you sad or angry you deliver energy to strengthen these dark angels. As they grow in strength and numbers they increase the misery on a planet. When we talk about living in a cloud of darkness we are referring to the swirling mists of despair that hinder all who live on Earth. It can be very difficult to see any facts clearly in a fog. So first, learn to detach from the emotional clouds of misery on Earth. Others have and so can you.

Let's say you've been practicing standing back and observing, learning to be balanced and neutral. How are your sadness levels now? They should have lowered as nothing is as bad as it is painted on Earth. From this position of lessened emotion you can start to look for the signs of light in your societies.

Light is kindness, dark is cruelty. Light is love, dark is hate. Light is truth, dark is lies. Light is joy, laughter and bliss, dark is misery and tears. Light is remembering the Creator Who Loves Us All, only love and never rejection. These qualities of light shine where they exist, they may be found side by side with darkness in a situation, but cannot be hidden. Light shines, it is hard to miss. When overhead the sky is dark you will still see the one white star. When you start looking unemotionally for the aspects of light in a situation you will find them and you will be able to judge for yourselves what is true or false.

Practicing finding the light in situations lets you build up a frame of reference for truth and lies. Specifically, how do they each feel to you? How do they feel different from each other? You have an inner core of light, how does truth make you feel, then the lies? There can be an acute reaction where you have to turn over a page in a newspaper and not look at someone's picture or turn off the radio or TV to avoid hearing the voice of someone lying to you. We recommend you avoid anyone who makes you feel like this. You are using your perception. You have rediscovered your truth sensors and are starting to use them, this will improve with practice. Avoiding the voice of someone lying to you in the news is self-preservation, you protect yourself from becoming angry at being lied to. It's insulting to your humanity.

One useful method to detach yourselves from useless angry emotions is to use a standard meditation technique. In meditation when a thought passes through your mind you acknowledge the thought but you don't engage. You don't go into a familiar pattern of angry thoughts about how awful a situation is or some political leaders are. Simply acknowledge the thought, let it go, and think about something else. This is the fastest way to let go of non-beneficial emotional patterns. As they vanish, you will find peace and restoration of the real you inside your head. We know humanity, you are a high vibrational soul of light and negative thoughts can make you physically and mentally ill. It's hard enough to live in an atmosphere of dark fog without having fog in your mind as well. When you create clarity and light in your mind you shine and burn away the fog around you. In this way you change the world for others.

27

What Do I Do With the Truth?

NOW THAT you've calmed down and see and feel the light of truth in different stories and situations, what do you do? Part of your job is to remember what's happened and is happening right now, another part is to tell no lies. Let's say you are in a mixed group of people who disagree with each other politically, something that can be found in every country today. Do you convince others that you are right because you remember and they don't? Maybe, but we would ask you to remember that many people are no longer listening, they are only talking to convince *you*. You need to hold fast to telling no lies yourself in all such conversations, not agreeing where you don't agree and not exaggerating your own side of the argument.

Isn't it possible to do more? By living truthfully in this way you will have acted on behalf of the light present in your own soul. You can only act for yourself on this planet. Some people may notice you and see there is another way to behave in an argument, however the main benefit from your actions for humanity comes later, when your light helps you across the finishing line to ascension. Every soul to cross that line helps those who follow. You will also be spreading light instead of darkness on your planet by such behaviour.

Many, many people on Earth right now feel they can fix everything that is wrong with human society if only everyone would listen to them and follow their plan. Most of these plans completely contradict each other. It's not about the plan, or who proposes it, or who has the power to implement a plan. It's about kindness, caring for each other, love and truth. This is all that matters now, it's the end of humanity's time on Earth and you need to demonstrate that you've all learned to live with love. This is the part of God that the dark angels are busy camouflaging, tricking humanity so you will miss the chance at ascension. You will each need to learn this for yourself in life. You can't learn it for someone else, although you can help them. Give them our books! That's why we wrote them, so they would be read and help people understand.

One by one we wish to see you strong in the truth. In spite of our words that your actions matter most for ascension, they will of course help others here and now. People are sorely in need of rational examples of behaviour, the calm voice that diffuses arguments, a voice that calls a spade a spade. When you identify a lie and say the truth, others will hear it on some level, truth is very powerful and difficult for most to deny. They may do nothing with the insight and barely be aware of what they just heard, but on the inside they will store it away. Later another person or two may make the same truthful observation and it will cause a shift in their behaviour and beliefs. You may think "why didn't they change when I first said it?" They weren't ready then, but your words helped to open a crack in their consciousness. Someone else was then able to plant a seed of truth. This is the biggest reason why you can help by speaking the truth when the opportunity arises, even when it seems no one is listening.

We appear to think that you will be able to detect the truth where others have failed; that's exactly what we mean! If you practice our exercises above and trust the wisdom and light within your soul, you will navigate your way through the lies. The lies are boulders of darkness waiting to trip you up. Truth is a pathway that rises towards the light, showing you the way and letting you walk up and over the hazards. Let your hearts and minds guide you.

28

No Forward Movement

IF YOU HAVE trained your truth sensors you are now blood hounds on the trail of truth. You could be feeling less anxious and more relaxed. You may have found that there is far more truth and light out there than you previously believed and that humanity is basically honest, loving and caring. This is indeed the true situation, and with a head cleared of fog you can restart your progress towards ascension. Every person who resumes walking forward clearly, steadily and purposefully creates this energy for everyone else. This progressive forward energy is patchy on Earth, but the more people who start walking forward create movement and flow. In the 1960s you had the Civil Rights Movement, so named because people moved together in the same direction to achieve their goals.

Your direction was chosen by you before you incarnated in your body for this lifetime. All of you arrived here determined to lead humanity into ascension , which is now only a few lifetimes away. When you look around at people you probably wonder what happened to the others who came here with you? You see no discernable forward movement and instead there is backward motion in many quarters with hate, aggression and unkindness levels on the rise. With so many determined souls on the planet to help the Earth and help humanity reach ascension why hasn't the entire population moved beyond this to greater peace and love? Why are there still wars? Sometimes it seems worse to us every day, although there are joyous expressions of love that pop up to be balanced against hate-filled actions. Has everyone forgotten why they're here?

Can you look at people who disagree with you and love them as much as those whose actions you approve? That is why you are on Earth, to know and express love in same way as the Creator. This is the ascension road, paved with love for all. By wearing a blindfold, humanity made this as hard as it could possibly be for a reason. If you could remember who you are after blinding yourself to nine higher dimensions, then there would be no point in another soul trying to find God by blindfolding themselves to eight, or five or two dimensions. It has the potential to tip the whole universe towards light and hasten the return to the Creator Who Loves Us All. You all hold the longing to return to this wholeness in the deepest part of your being. If you could learn to love under these difficult circumstances then anyone on any planet in the universe could do the same, and these lessons about love would be learned on behalf of All. You took this on yourself, it was actually your idea and the Earth trusted you to be able to carry out the plan. The core of light in humanity is strong, you may not detect it in the people on the news, but you will find it in your friends and neighbours. Even those who vote differently from you have the same shared humanity. You are so strong in light that even those who hate cannot stop humanity ascending.

Do the haters have a role that helps you all ascend? They have the same core but their actions are divisive rather than helping everyone join together as one soul. They genuinely make it harder for the greater human soul by distracting others from the pathway of love. It's also harder to find love when you are under attack. Opportunities are created to step forward and learn about caring for those in need of help. There are many destitute people and refugees on your planet today and their numbers will continue to rise before they begin to fall. It is a great opportunity to practice love and to put yourself in the shoes of others. But it was never a necessary step in your growth right now, you are repeating a lesson you have learned in your past. As you are repeating the lesson anyway, get the most out of it by practicing caring for others with love. With the upcoming Earth changes there will be even more refugees.

The times that are upon you now will create large patterns of movement across the globe because of the Earth's need to evolve. She is hanging on to her self-control with her fingertips because of climate change. It would be helpful if there was planning taking place right now for the people who will be forced to move from their homes because their land has been made uninhabitable. It will be the great challenge of your time to treat others as you would be treated yourself, sharing so that everyone has enough. A time of leaving the planet is starting now, as many will say goodbye and go home to rejoin the human soul.

29

Earth Changes

THE EARTH has changed a great deal since 2012. In December of that year she was reborn as a new planet, flashing in and out of existence so quickly very few noticed it happening at the time. That was the instant she was ready to step into her new future in a higher dimension, but she needed to maintain a physical presence for those who were not ready and still call her home. She raised her vibrational level over a matter of a few months and began to exist only at the new level. The old Earth, at its old vibrational level came to an end and the new level is where the future lies today. Those who did not choose to raise their vibration when she raised hers, and everyone had the choice offered to them, do not have the sustenance of her former energy to keep them going. It's as if they are trying to breath a poisonous atmosphere no longer suited to their bodies. These people will eventually run out of energy and their ability to cope with the new Earth. For the most part these are the people who only value the treasures they have in this lifetime, never thinking beyond power or possessions.

Earth changes are now lined up, one after another, to set her free from the three dimensional limits required while humanity has been resident here. The changes will happen in a sequence that is similar to a pinball machine; first a hit on one place, then bouncing to another across the globe, then pinging back to hit more locations. She will attempt to slow it down between hits but she can't stop it until it has run its course. For the Earth these are overdue self-corrections, like shaking out a leg that started to cramp from sitting still too long. Shaking and stretching will return her to equilibrium, as she did not expect there to be solid life forms resident when the time for changes arrived. The non-human lives on Earth (plants, animals, insects, etc.) are already living on a higher energy plane, ready to move with her into the higher dimensions. The time has come for these changes to take place.

One of a pattern of universal waves that passed through in October 2018 was aimed at helping Earth (and other planets) shake off the build up of crud accumulated over eons. First the energy arrives, then the unstoppable physical changes will begin to take place. This detoxing process of the Earth was planned as part of a galaxy-wide cleanse deep in the past, to take place before the universe stopped expanding and turned back towards the Source of All. The fact that humanity wasn't ready to ascend with everyone else makes them stand out on Earth now. If you look around at the energy of your surroundings it is buzzing with life, until you gaze upon a solid human. They are clearly of a separate vibration and easy to see in their density against a background of moving energy.

Earth will do her best to care for the human lives on her surface, and the greater human soul is helping by bringing home those whose time is up. Normally we do not like to imply that any tiny part of God is better or worse than any other part, because it is simply not true. However the actions of some humans present on Earth are having an affect on the overall vibration of light on the planet, which is challenging for the whole of humanity. We are positive that, given endless time, humanity would have again found their soul of light through karma and an ever-increasing speed of individual ascensions. Also there are some trends towards the light that would have changed society over time, such as using the internet for the purposes of enlightening and uniting people. Everyone came to Earth to do the best they could on behalf of the light, but some have never lived the lives they originally intended. They will go home to the greater human soul and learn the lessons they didn't learn while they were alive on Earth, while the remaining resident humans will be free to learn about oneness and start healing the planet without continual obstruction. The human soul has made this decision for itself.

Planets in this galaxy were blown over onto their sides by the force of the waves of energy in October 2018, shaking them free of their accumulated pasts, cleaning them off and preparing them for their return to The Creator Who Loves Us All. Earth and some other planets benefited from additional help with stabilisation and the waves blew through each molecule and back into the universe. Mars underwent a real buffeting while bracing against the energy and resisting the flow, resulting in less energy flooding through. Crystals deep inside the Earth formed into healing crystal grids to guide the energy through the planet and funnel it out. What used to look like solid rock now flows freely like sand, bright with light.

Every part of the Earth was flooded with universal energy, over and over again until she was recharged with ever increasing and higher energy. This is no longer the same planet, it's energy has been renewed. Energy is more important in the life of any being than the physical body. Earth is ready to move, shake, jump and dance.

The October 2018 energy came in two waves, the first had the effect of hitting your buildings and social structures at the higher dimensions and weakening them, cracking them as if loosening great chunks of falling masonry. The second wave energetically flattened all this to the ground. First the energy changes, followed by the physical changes. It's good to remember that if you want life to go on as before, unchanged, that it is never really possible in a forward travelling universe. After such a massive energy change, life will be rebuilt from the ground up. Nothing can remain the same following the two waves. Instead we will see new growth rising between the cracks where the old buildings and structures once were. What will you build in their place?

The Earth can't stop her own forward progress, she can only slow it down and only then for a short space of time. The human soul knows this and has fine-tuned some of the rules of the game, helping itself by rearranging its players. Like a good sports team manager does., it is completely in control and can pull players off the field, while substituting new ones to try to win the game. Look for some big changes taking place around death and dying.

The babies that are being born on Earth post- 2012 are the strongest and most determined human beings the human soul can place on the planet. Tiny babies of love and strength are being born and all are of one mind and have the same goals. It doesn't matter which continent a baby is born on, they will push back against attempts to ruin the planet. They will resist killing their fellow humans because a political boss ordered them to, and they will refuse to neglect the unfortunate. These babies are primed to complete the lessons that humanity needs to finally learn before ascension. If everyone does their best to help the young and help the planet, then they are doing exactly what is needed. Don't worry about the future of humanity, we believe you will ascend and help the rest of the universe through your actions. It won't be many more decades now.

Part Four
Lift Off!

30

Azreal, the Archangel of Death

THERE WAS a time when we angels could visit you and you would see us, we could walk with you and laugh together. People asked us questions and we dropped wisdom into their hearts like fresh rainwater after a drought. This manner of personal teaching was abandoned in Atlantis when deception and impersonation by our dark brethren became harmful and confusing. Humanity participated in drawing the veils between our two kinds.

Later we visited you in dreams and inspired your writing and music. The churches intervened to punish the dreamers and the messages could not be spoken. Music remained and if you find that there are pieces of music that uplift your being, often we have gifted the music of the spheres, the music of love, to the composer. Today we are taking advantage of human technology to speak through writings on the internet, dictate channelled books like this one, appear on channelled webcasts and recorded talks. When a message is uplifting and informative and touches your heart, it is most likely inspired by the half of the universe that is love.

In the past specially trained people preached this information formally in temples, today those disseminating our words are many and informal. The ability and talent to channel is reawakening among many and there are many voices now where there were once few. They are our mouthpieces and once again we are giving you raindrops of life after a long drought. This is happening today because of the events taking place on Earth among people and other life forms. Now is the time for action and we are trying to help guide you without words on a pathway for the highest universal good.

In this book we have discussed Truth and we have discussed Death, because misunderstanding the truth has scrambled your ideas about death. Each of you will reach the end of this life one day and die, and we are most concerned about the manner of your going. We see the dawning realisation in people's minds when they know they will soon die, and we witness the shock and fear present ninety-nine percent of the time. There have been many great teachers over the ages who preached to you about love, but few listeners have fully understood what a universe created in love means to them personally. The overwhelming love that is the background to life never means you harm, even in death. Death is an expected part of life and the love and care for each one of you doesn't end when your physical body dies. Love desires to alleviate fear, as fear dampens your pleasure in life. Love assists you to find joy and comfort every day you are alive.

For this reason, I, Azreal, the Archangel of Death am here in these pages to help lessen the fear surrounding death for all those who read this book. When we angels write a book the words are ours, and they carry the energy that we intend them to carry. You may be reading them on paper or electronic media, but it is our energy that you are taking in. As long as you don't deliberately block the energy or the message you will begin the process of change from fear to love. When each of you changes, the energy on the planet shifts a little. If you can personally approach the end of your life with the knowledge that death is not the end, or a place of eternal torment or nothingness, then instead of fear you will have acceptance. After all, no one on Earth lives in one body forever and you are aware of this. In ages past you laid yourselves down surrounded by loved ones and said "I am content to go now. When it is your turn, be content also." Afterwards you awake as if from a dream of owning a body and living on Earth. You are once again conscious and have full possession of your mind and the wisdom of your soul.

In the past you knew that this is how life and death are bound together, and, buried deep inside, you still have that knowledge. Now is the time to relax and centre your thoughts in your heart and ask your higher self if this book is true. Your higher self is another way of describing your soul, it is the complete soul without veils and is available to you during meditation. Here you are in all your wisdom and complexity, wise with knowledge gained over years of living on planets. You are alive in all dimensions and have a connection to your terrestrial human heart. One day when you die you will again be this wise soul, just without a connection to a physical body.

Angels rarely have bodies. When we incarnate on a planet like Earth we need to work with the greater human soul (if we are using human bodies, not dolphins, whales, birds or other life forms) and receive its permission to be born as a baby. As angels and humans are each souls of light this is not too difficult to arrange. We are born and forget everything exactly as if we are human, we go on to find our path in life just as you do and this can be as difficult for us as for any human. We are human for our entire lifetime on Earth and that can present both problems and gifts for us; it is a gift to experience being as creative as you are. Creativity is the aspect of the Creator that we are all most aware of, for He created all of us. We consider you our siblings, our family and we work to help you reach your goals. We play our roles in the universe generally without bodies, while humans incarnate on planets. Angels do not get karmically "stuck" on Earth, they reincarnate over and over to help humanity and the Earth. Dedicated angels are valued experts and often incarnate and work on behalf of the planet, as Earth is a valued sister to all life in the universe.

At this time on Earth you will find more incarnate angels than ever before. We are here to help, to get our hands dirty cleaning the planet or perhaps by sitting in dull meetings trying to get more environmental protection laws in place. We do it because you are family, Earth is family, and you both need to last a little while longer to finish your contracts. The day you all ascend the Earth will reform herself at a higher vibration and life will be adjusted to her new form. Humanity will be here along with every other species that signed up for the next phase. At the moment she is like a box bursting with light, where we have to sit on the lid to keep it from lifting off for a little while longer. So far we have helped her to keep her lid on and her physical form remains the same as it has been these long ages. We are all rather excited by the next phase arriving soon due to her energy and her commitment to the light. We are waiting for lift off!

31

Crop Circles

EVERY DAY big changes for humanity creep closer, your game here now appears, from our perspective, that it will be completed soon. This means that whether humanity is ready or not, when the time is up either you will have ascended or you will admit defeat. We do not tell you the day or year. We know that there is a new feeling of determination, a let's-get-on-with-it energy flowing through humanity these days. This energy is what was missing in the past and is only here now because you are substituting and changing your team players. When people die now it is because either their souls are tired, or they have finished their lessons for this life, or they are causing more harm than good in the progress to ascension. Please do not try to guess which is which. Keep your trust in the greater human soul; it knows what it is doing and from its timeless viewpoint makes decisions based on all the facts. Your opinion of who is the worst human being on the planet may not be the person that is actually doing the most harm. Even if they were proved to be the worst, they are still a part of you and a part of God. Trust yourself, trust the human soul.

All living beings are energy, energy that has slowed down into a physical form. You are always part of the flow of energy and as you move with it and blend with it you become familiar with its properties. You are part of the complicated story of Earth and you can all feel the end point for humanity like a knot in the ribbon of flow. Everyone could feel the end and rebirth of the Earth in 2012, but most chose to ignore that feeling. When you know something in your heart and it is mentioned to you, you will remember and it feels right. The team of lightworkers present on Earth today are teaching and reminding others about cosmic truths. Truth is very hard to deny when you already know it is true inside your heart. Nevertheless, some always do.

You all have an inner awareness that there is a finite time span for this phase of the Earth, and you can all feel the closeness of the approaching change. That is the motivation for the human soul to make these comprehensive and serious changes. Never before has it called part of itself home to achieve forward motion. They do so now because right when humanity had hoped there would be a greater understanding that all beings are one, you once again headed into reverse. So many hate others for so many reasons at the moment, that the human soul is stepping in to say "This is not why we came here! If you can't treat each other with love, you will have to sit in the corner and wait. Time's up for you, you're coming home." This is never intended as a punishment but instead aims to remove obstacles to success. The human soul is acting swiftly in the time remaining, before it is too late to take any action.

A long time ago the length of a human life on Earth was not defined by a number of years or centuries but measured only by the soul's learning. As this game was being put into place and then was up and running, the rest of the universe did not stand still and wait for it to finish. You have been here for a much longer period of time than was ever dreamed of, and have taken so many false steps that you are not quite yet close enough to the end. However, in the rest of the universe there has been a lot of progress and some of it has been based on the supposition that humanity will pull off this challenging game. Just the idea of the success of your game has been enough to lead other beings forward, and forward they went! What if you fail to ascend after all? In some ways it won't matter in the bigger picture, but it will matter to humanity. The rest of the universe is waiting at a much higher level than it had reached before, they have learned by watching your mistakes here. These other planets are calmer and more peaceful than the warlike and chaotic Earth. They hold light more strongly by assuming you will also reach the next step to ascension. You have provided light for others that you do not enjoy yourself.

These other planets and stars are building on your proposed success, they jumped over the intervening steps and carried on rising and they want to show you how you helped them, and help you in return. This is a universe of love as much as a universe of hate and we are saying here for the first time that you have helped bring love and peace to others far away from Earth. They consider you as one with themselves and feel your fear and pain as they stand by to help. These are the "aliens" some speak of, they are the star beings of the universe. Beings of light do not interfere on Earth, but they watch events unfolding; you can find their words on the internet channelled by others. Take what you believe to be true and leave the rest. Use your discernment when it comes to each and every channel, to only take what seems true for you.

Some of the star beings that are popularly channelled owe their advanced planetary societies to you. You and your creativity showed them a new way to learn, you provided a higher jumping off point for them to begin their new experiences. You also provided examples of misery for them to avoid. Earth is protected now and those beings who previously landed and kidnapped citizens for their own learning are kept out by us and others. When any of them come near they can't get through our barriers of light. This is useful to remember when you discuss colonizing Mars, is this something you have the right to do? Mars has its own population and they have the first say in what happens there. If you were aware of more than three dimensions you would see them in the background of all the photos taken on Mars. Yours are the alien spaceships there.

Crop circles are formed by the Earth, by aliens and by demons. Can you tell the difference or do you see them all as being the same? We are very fond of crop circles, they provide unsolved puzzles for you. Your establishments try to divert your attention away from them so they don't have to explain something they don't understand. Go with what you intuitively think and feel. Study the photos of the ones that speak to you as they are a means of communication. What do they say to you? There is a sense of joy associated with many of the crop circles, they are fun to create and the joy lingers. Beware of any that do not carry the energy of light and stay out of them. They are the copycat circles created by demons and their purpose is to harm you with their energy. Use your intuition.

Crop circles are formed where they can be easily seen on large, cultivated fields. These fields are in areas where the energy skin on the Earth is thin and her energy is most available. She is able to project the image of her symbol from the inside, it travels outwards and can be read as a pattern of light as far away as the opposite side of your galaxy. She is communicating with far more than the beings on her surface. Forming these patterns is how the Earth and the star beings play with each other, like drawing pictures in sand. What star beings see as a symbol of light they are able to help manifest on Earth. These beings are unseen in your three dimensions, forming crop circles is reaching through the dimensions into your existence on Earth and is intended to help humanity's consciousness expand. The internet has many pictures of crop circle these days and we suggest you look at them and see if they have something to say to you.

Crop circles contain pieces of information, a phrase or even a complex formula in the form of a symbol. Symbols can be intuitively read by some, perhaps you are one of the readers yourself? Sitting with a picture of a crop circle while meditating is the best way to begin to understand and read them. Symbols are a form of passing information from one being to another, and some symbols are active and meant to be absorbed through your aura and used. Others are simply to be read. They are a universal shorthand, much quicker than writing out long explanations or doing spells and incantations.

Some of you will be familiar with the active symbols used in Reiki, as well as different symbols used in other forms of healing. If you use symbols already you know that somehow they work, producing an expected result. Look back over pictures from years of crop circles and see what you can learn from them.

Symbols allow a free-flowing river of information to travel around the galaxy and beyond. The Earth is part of this flow and symbols are present here now in great quantities. They arrived and settled into people's auras and are slowly working their way into becoming part of their energy. If you had no affinity for a symbol, it moved on looking for someone else to make a good fit. When you connected with an appropriate symbol it enhanced your skills and intuition. You were upgraded in the areas where you already had an interest and they are helping you pursue it. This is easiest to understand with scientists, where a symbol could help lead to a breakthrough in research, or point someone in a brand-new direction. They are only what they are: a means for communicating ideas or an active key. In Reiki they can "open a door" to using the energy in different helpful ways for healing. They make healing more targeted and provide for distant healing and healing the subconscious mind.

Can crop circles provide healing symbols like the Reiki symbols? There have been one or two that have double uses, one of which was for healing. Giving healing symbols without explanations or training is not often successful. Most crop circles provide messages for humanity. Simplified, the messages are along the lines of "You are not alone, look at what we made here for you. Have fun studying it."

32

Star Beings

HUMANITY has many, many brothers and sisters in the universe. Your siblings were formed at the exact same time as you by the Creator, made to take a variety of physical forms on planets and learn what it is to be a tiny part of God. In your many planetary experiences you have sometimes been alone on a planet as the single soul group. Most often humanity has been with different beings for each game, and rarely do you repeat time with a soul group. Instead it is most common to meet new souls, learning more about yourselves in that way. Your experience on Earth has a huge number of the original siblings present amongst others in the insect, animal, mineral, bacteria kingdoms. These souls could design any form to experience life on Earth and have appeared as they are now to learn lessons of their own choosing. We know some humans barely see other people as being the same species, but we mention this sibling relationship now so you will redouble your efforts to save all these others from extinction. You protect these beings to demonstrate that you are living your best version of yourself and to show you value all that the Creator has made. Killing siblings has a strong taboo in human society, we see the way you have killed on this planet and we are sad for you. One day you will wake up and be horrified at your actions and it will take some time to come to terms with them. You are all star beings together.

Off-planet visitors, from the different worlds in the Milky Way Galaxy, have been learning on planets in the same way as you. They were at varied levels in learning their purpose as a soul when humanity started this advanced game on Earth. When their planetary games finished and they were planning their next adventure they took a look at what was happening on Earth. They needed to plan for success on Earth (for when has humanity ever failed in the past?) and pitch their game a degree higher. This was done as if you had achieved the near impossible: remembering who you are while blindfolded and ignorant of absolutely everything. These games started while you were far from finished here, overlapping your efforts. Some of them completed those games and embarked on new ones to learn even more. The universe didn't stop when you ran into trouble, instead it carried this energy forward. Your efforts are appreciated by all, you took the lead and others followed on parallel pathways. Today some of them are truly superior societies of love and they are very grateful for all you are doing.

What makes a superior society? It's not by acquiring more powerful weapons or technology, it is by stretching out and holding ever greater quantities of love. Those star beings who speak through other channels give help and advice to sooth the fear and pain of being human. They are concerned that people's emotional wounds will lead to greater physical damage. Most of your home grown shooters and mass murderers are wounded and damaged people; we off-planet beings can all detect their pain. Star beings would like to help everyone in pain but can only help within parameters that are set by the greater human soul. They can offer guidance, but not interfere. The human soul is aware that it has almost completed its time here. The other planets are prepared for that moment and the galactic shift will happen everywhere at once. Need I say we angels have found all of this fascinating and an honour to participate in this with you?

A galactic shift to light will involve a lot of life moving together at once towards the Creator Who Loves Us All. Is the whole universe going home at that time? If it is only this galaxy shifting it still contributes to the universal flow and movement towards light. Other galaxies will feel the change in energy, it will support those galaxies as they have supported the Milky Way in the past. Everything that flows helps the ascension process. If something is backwards or stagnant it holds everything back while flow is eased into being again. When you are presented with opportunities to act, or vote and you are trying to decide what is best to do, look for flow or stagnancy as part of the picture. Taking societies back to the "good old days" is not possible and is never a good idea. Take them instead into the future.

Because the star beings' societies are advanced and loving they hold this love energy for this planet and others. These provide a background of love for the Earth and that has been very supportive over the millennia you have been here. There is a galaxy full of your siblings holding the energy of love for you and everything else. This is a great benefit, and it is partly due to your risky game contributing to other planets' development. Everything is intertwined and nothing exists in a vacuum. You have contributed something of great value through your long (and we mean LONG!) ages here on Earth. This is culminating in a fierce desire of humanity to wrap this game up and get it over with. That is why people are going to die when their timers go off and they return home.

33

Neither Male nor Female

D ID EVERY human wear a timer in the past and return home when their time was up? These timers were a new introduction from the beginning of 2018. Previously the length of time any soul was incarnate on Earth was decided by that individual soul, not the collective human soul. This is a big innovation. During each life time a person was learning to judge when they had reached the correct time and way to leave the planet, easily and peacefully. It was a step towards learning control while realising that the Creator has the ultimate control, and that you are the Creator in your life. Now the greater human soul has learned from all these individuals about when and how to die and it is shifting to learn something new. The greater human soul is dynamic and ever-changing, it is always adjusting itself one or two steps ahead of the actions on Earth.

These changes happen all the time with planetary games. Everyone comes onto Earth with plans to live their life while learning; and when the lessons are learned it is more efficient to release the physical body and return with a new plan. We make it sound like this is easy, but people know how much they will be missed and there is so much fear and sadness around death from both the young who remain and the old who die. Would it help if you knew that the one transitioning is living according to their plan? That you are also living according to your plan and that the only thing really important to you is successfully completing that plan? Nothing ever stays the same, everything is always changing.

Humanity is showing not only itself, but the entire universe that enough individuals are rising to the light and ascending now to complete this game. They are the people who have learned who they really are and they are helped to ascend by everyone who ascended before them. And the others who are destroying the planet? They helped many to ascend by providing a focal point and demonstrating the qualities you do not want to take forward. But you have more of this kind of person than you need right now and their wealth and power is a crushing weight for the rest of you to cope with. It makes it too hard, it could take too long.

The greater human soul can be seen like a team running a spaceship, sitting at a consol and making decisions to keep the ship going forward. Your team has almost eight billion souls working together to keep the forward momentum. Everyone has a role, everyone has a say, no one is less than another. This oneness of soul has turned into division and strife on Earth. Fighting yourself has stalled forward movement for thousands of years. All wars are about power and possessions; who will wield the power? It's been done over and over and is useless now as something new to learn and take back. The timers are a direct intervention in direction, changing from lessons already learned to something new. Death can be used to rebalance human society. It releases people and helps them to leave when their lives are over and not continue living on through fear.

With this intervention humanity is turning a corner while still going forward. Your time here isn't finished yet, not for years, and there are many more changes to come. This is not the only big change on the horizon for you, but it is the change that is starting now.

Death is one aspect of human life that is now quite out of balance. When one part is as unbalanced as the human relationship to death currently is, there is a knock-on effect on every aspect of your lives. To rebalance death as a part of life the greater human soul is drawing home those who have completed their lives but remained active on Earth. This is now seen as a necessary step. Humanity has finished various lessons, such as those to do with over-population and environmental destruction. Those who are still taking harmful decisions affecting the rest of you are often those who have finished their lives and are therefore disengaged from the Earth. One such decision recently was to dump radioactive sludge in the Bristol Channel in the UK, near the large population centres of South Wales. Those making a decision like this have no personal energy, they are like the dead walking. Your own greater soul is helping you all return to balance and the biggest imbalance is hanging onto lives past the time they have finished. We know that many who are here are loved and loving, and they will be missed when they die. It is always the way when people die that they are remembered and missed, it is this love that makes you a part of the Creator Who Loves Us All.

Beginning now and ending when the population balances, people will begin to die at an increasing rate. Every family may be touched by these deaths and be led to a greater understanding of what happens when someone dies. We do not wish to sound heartless, and we are truly sorry for all who suffer loss and pain.

Reducing the world's population is a theme that has been recurring for centuries and is currently a plotline in works of fiction and films. Invoking "For the Greater Good" villains often wish to kill others on a vast scale. In these plots there are a few individual souls who decide to kill the many to give themselves more of everything on Earth. This is not what we are talking about. When each of you is born you pre-selected your learning targets and when you achieve them you have finished, although there are always exceptions to every rule. If you choose to remain because you love your family or your life, no one is going to drag you away. If you are remaining because you are greedy and hurting others, accumulating more and more possessions, then you are probably wearing a timer on your chest. If you are remaining because you finished but are afraid to die and don't know what is coming next, there is help for you. Timers take the effort out of dying. There is no more agonizing over letting go and walking through the doorway to home. There is a loving escort and care for each person who dies. Timers are ticking for many today as there are many "overdue" deaths. For those who are hurting others, the energy has already changed and their actions are no longer aligned with it, there is no longer a place for them on Earth.

This book about death is intended to help you overcome your fear of what comes next. Your extremely restricted game on Earth led you to forget your true selves. Earthly life is the dream; when you are back in spirit you will be fully conscious once again, busy and active, sharing and making plans with others. What do you want to do in your next life? Your desire will be to bring the entire soul forward towards the light by your actions while on Earth. We see that for a great many of you this is exactly what you are managing to do even though you are rarely conscious of your plans.

We honour you for the determination and effort you all put into your lives. There are some whose lives shine and shoot straight forward like an arrow from the bow. The Ascended Master Mozart was one of these, we can still see the trail of stars left behind after his life's brief journey showing others how to incorporate light into music. These are people of great determination who have planned risky lives, often pinning an entire incarnation on one aspect of living. They go straight for their target and don't diverge from the path. If you know one of these people then don't get in their way, they are helping all of you with their achievements. If you think about it you will be able to find some examples of these people from your news stories.

Earlier we wrote about life and the flow of existence you experience after you are dead. It's not sitting on a cloud with a harp, singing, walking through the Elysian fields or crossing the river Styx. When you leave your body behind you are offered the opportunity to rest, even animals have a rest between lives. Resting calms the mind and prepares you to ease back into life once again following death. You recall the life just completed and consider your successes and the parts you'd like to live over. Then you remember all your previous lives and add the latest experiences to the overall picture. For example, all the lessons you've learned about being a mother are added together. Some of these experiences of being human you have completed now and when next alive you will not need to repeat them. When you meet those who say "I don't plan to have children" they could be those who don't need that experience again. You are in a period where many who are not planning to have any children have incarnated, after all, you have been here so long that most of you have ticked the parenthood box. There will still be those having babies because children are great teachers and joy bringers. Children will continue to be part of humanity's life here.

The plan for your next life will be developed after wide-ranging discussions with other souls. You will be looking for those who can help you with the parts you wish to repeat, and they are looking for the same help from you. After a while you have your next team together and the details are worked out. Details such as where is the best place to live to have the experiences you need. This could literally be anywhere on the planet. In a large country like the USA, the region will be chosen to provide you with a suitable background for learning. For example, there are big cultural differences between Texas and Maine. One will provide the most suitable background.

By choosing your birth location you have put into place some of the forces that will shape you before you are even born. This increases your chances of having the experiences you need to really understand who you are, imagine not having to deal with the difficulties provided by overcoming the wrong culture. A few people are parachuted in to random families if they need to be on Earth to do a specific job on behalf of the whole. If you did appear just anywhere on the planet, you could find the cultural details missing that would bring you the learning you needed in this life. How wise it was of humanity to ensure a wide variety of cultures to provide all these experiences!

What about the people who are born into impoverished third-world countries? Nelson Mandela was born into a white supremacist society with his brown skin; where did he get his support from to keep himself moving forward and continue learning? His job was so hard that he needed the support of many, and the group that agreed to incarnate into poverty with him in South Africa was enormous. When those souls agreed to incarnate into poverty they were proud to be part of a necessary change. No one dropped out after thinking about what their impoverished life would actually be like to live, planetary lives are so short here compared to your immortal soul. Most by now have led lives of poverty, been members of all the skin colour groups, as well as both sexes.

We watch as your young people today experiment with new sexual identities. They have had many previous lives as male or female and they have finished learning what they needed to know as either or both. They are now shattering the notion that there is nothing but men or women. A long time ago in Atlantis you divided into male and female in a use of energy that altered the lives of almost every species on the planet. This is a rule of life on Earth right now, but it is dissolving, shifting. An old Earth pattern is being released that is not replicated in the wider universe and will not serve you as you rejoin galactic life. This is an exciting, fundamental shift on your world. You are eye-witnesses to change at the deepest level. First the energy changed, then your youth began to let go of fixed sexes. Why don't they pick a sex and stick to it? Because the energy is not remotely fixed, it flows and they are feeling the flow. It sways them back and forth like seaweed and allows them to experiment and learn about life without a fixed sex. It has been a very long time since humanity was neither male nor female and this is being revisited now by some of you. The few leading the way will increase in numbers as time goes by.

Experimentation with fluid sexual identity does not exist in a vacuum that only affects young people. It affects their families and is slowly rippling outwards as the energy grows stronger. Fluid sexuality changes human identity and the way you see yourselves here, it requires you to adapt to these young people or block them. If you obstruct, you harm them and some will become mentally ill or die. Every generation has something to offer and this is a courageous gift, it only needs to be accepted to expand the idea of what it is to be human.

You believe that the elderly lead the world societies, but this is only true in material wealth and positions of power. World leaders are truly the young, who lead you forward into understanding the current energy. In the 1960s the energy changed and young people wanted to leave behind their parents' way of living. That was the point of it all, any of you could have learned from them, left your pasts behind and walked forward freely into a new way of life. Society's past is where you've been stuck and the future is always coming closer with its forecast changes in energy. Life is always easier when aligned with the prevailing energy.

34

Walk-Ins

ULTIMATELY, the universe is a place of flowing energy. You have been managing to live and learn on Earth in an energy of almost stasis. Perhaps you might think: what about the rocks, they don't move? And yet, they also move and flow around the Earth. You consider their movement slow, but they do not. They regard it as fast enough to learn about flow across the surface of the Earth, creating new continents and sinking old ones. They have learned about structure, support and when to let go and give way. It's in letting go where humanity is stuck these days, but all will be learned in the end. If you, as a single individual, learn to release and drop everything that keeps your energy from flowing, then you too will flow. At that point you will be moving towards ascending to the light when next in spirit form. Naturally your behaviour will have altered to reflect your understanding while still alive here and others will have taken note. You are setting a good example and when others copy you they too will be learning to flow. This is how the process of ascension will speed up, as one person at a time embraces the flow of energy in their lives. Spontaneity is something that you can practise.

Who's on the ascension pathway in this life? There are many these days, in ever increasing numbers. They were deliberately born here now for just this reason, as many of you only need to learn how to let go and flow as a last lesson in life. These people are already close to ascension and, by incarnating many at once, they create momentum and help for others. When they are finished they will have a choice: to either come back or stay home and be a spirit guide for others. We find that there are always a few that will come back to Earth. The rest are holding the energy of ascension as a tight core group within the human soul. It's very beneficial to you all that this group exists and holds this energy of light. One day the entire human soul will be part of this group.

A long time ago one of your great teachers talked about separating the sheep from the goats. This is another process that is coming into play now and when some finish living they will be separated and held back from embarking on their next lifetime. When the entire population *alive on the planet* has realised they are part of God all humanity will ascend together.

You will notice in the coming years on Earth an increased rate of change along with increasingly large changes. There are no restrictions to the changes, who will change or where the changes will be. The Earth herself is able to change and, as shown in Atlantis, events can happen very quickly. Societies can mutate and alter in a few short years and there is no returning to the past. Always there must be forward motion, finding a new way to learn lessons and solve problems. We will say that as humanity has completed so many of its planned objectives by now that it is likely to go deeper into a situation, and have fewer dramatic scenarios. For instance, your political regimes are more likely to mimic each other and there will be fewer models of government. A case in point is that Communism has almost completely disappeared, even the large communist country of China operates as a hybrid with Capitalism.

There will be a noticeable increase in the number of deaths in the elderly. These are people for whom the right time to leave has arrived, or those who missed their time and remained on Earth through fear of death. There are many elderly who are ready to leave that are physically and mentally infirm. There are younger people who are ready to leave and swiftly return with a new plan. You will find that these younger people have been building an entire series of life plans in their rest periods back with the human soul. Reincarnations are speeding up in a deliberate, designed manner to bring ascension closer. In order for this to happen plans have to be made. There will be more "walk-ins", where one person surrenders a body to another so that two lives can complete their plans in the quickest possible way. When this is the plan it is created in advance of the life and care is taken not to disrupt third party lives. It will be done in a discreet way, usually for those not in a relationship.

"Walk-ins" have always taken place on Earth among humans, and it is a tightly controlled event. Other soul changes can be along the lines of "upgrades" where a greater amount of the soul's wisdom is incorporated. In this lifetime it is easier to download more of a person's soul when that soul is not in a body. In this case the soul is whipped out of the body, upgraded, and put back in very quickly. It is a rebirth-same-body and results in a change of birth chart, for those interested in astrology. It is a true death and rebirth, similar to that of the Earth is 2012. It can take up to two years to adjust after such a rebirth, unless a highly skilled healer is present to help. We will then work through the healer to assist with the adjustment.

In any of these soul changes we angels work as midwives, we simply help with the process by providing healing energy, secure any boundaries against interference, and provide peace. It is a human event, not angelic.

35

The Immortality of Your Soul

DEATH is viewed in many ways and none of them are true unless they acknowledge your immortal soul. Immortality is the key that unlocks the reality of your continued existence. There are those who believe that there is only this one life and when it ends there is no further existence, just nothing. When you accept immortality you can then begin to ponder the larger questions of why any of you have a soul and why you are here? What is your purpose? If you believe that you are briefly alive, then dead with nothing beyond this one life, again, what is your purpose? It would be small and lightweight, almost without any point to it at all. It makes humanity correspondingly small, and this soul group is not small, it is weighty with experience and life.

Any belief that teaches there is no point to life or no afterlife is a trick, it's a road leading away from love for yourself and others. It opens a door to mistreating all other life forms on the planet because there is no responsibility for your actions, if you are only here one day and gone the next. It this were really true where does the sense of responsibility come from that is at the core of loving, human behaviour? The greater majority of people are decent, kind and loving and this is an expression of your soul's wisdom. You've relearned most of what you need to know about the nature of God through observation of how people act, and you express this knowledge as kind and loving behaviour. You should all be proud of this.

The nature of the Creator Who Loves Us All is not unfathomable. It is illustrated by the people around you every day on Earth. It is love deeper than you can experience in your short lives but it is also the opposite. A tyrant expresses brutality and that is also part of the nature of the Creator. Do you choose to live as a tyrant and express cruelty? Then you are choosing the vibrations of darkness and misery and all vibrations come from the single Source. Does the One who is all loving deliberately hurt his own creations? It is allowed within the rules of your universe of polarity. It expands the heights of bliss and the depths of sorrow by allowing a deepening of experience and knowledge to be gained. The only choice you need to make is living in joy or living in misery. Reach out, or reach into your hearts, to find your Creator and you will begin to touch the Source of love and joy. Bring it into your lives and those who meet you will notice on some level. Popular people tend to carry these vibrations, people normally can't get enough of the vibration of love. Human beings are born from a soul of light and living surrounded by darker vibrations makes life harder for each one of you.

What will Earth be like with fewer people, will it ever be able to recover its health and beauty? Well, yes! Think of an area you know that has been over-exploited and ruined and is now unable to support life. At the moment there are too many of these places in the world. If you picture a dead coral reef, lifeless with only a few fish and marine animals, imagine looking at it again in fifty years. If during this time no humans have interfered with the reef through acid rain, dredging, fishing, boating or any of the other things humans do to oceans, there will be recovery. The marine elementals can help with the energy on the reef to promote growth and health. They are present at these reefs right now trying to hold them together, if possible, stretched to the limit by their efforts to protect and help the oceans. They are currently set back more rapidly than they can move forward in their work.

If the reef were left alone it could be remade by the Earth, the ocean dwellers and the marine elementals. A blueprint exists as the underlying foundation for a paradise Earth and all life desires to go back to that pattern. The pathway back into the original plan is much easier to find than trying to resist the blueprint. As in the oceans, there are many places on the land that could recover relatively quickly, and there are other places that will take a very long time. For this reason we urge you to fight against nuclear waste dumping, and fracking. Fracking is hugely destructive where it occurs by breaking down the structure of the Earth itself. It is still in its infancy and it is too early to see how long it will take the land to fully recover. There are alternative methods of providing energy on Earth more natural than this destructive and greedy practice. In a few short years it will disappear from use and if you can resist it now the areas destroyed will be fewer. Resist this practice, so disrespectful to the planet that gives you a home.

Death is a part of your soul's journey, it marks the end of working towards ascension while in a dreamlike state in a physical body. When you wake from this life by passing through death's door, your soul regains consciousness. Reunited with your human soul group you exist in the light, in a state of happiness and purpose. You are inventive and determined, creative with your planning and risk-taking. What would be considered self-sacrifice on Earth is just life and an expression of love when you are Home. You are never lonely, as the walls between each of you become so thin that you are aware of only what you have in common and never see any differences. You share with pleasure and delight, generous with your accumulated knowledge. Living in a physical body is the only way to gain experience and you bravely submit yourselves to one life after another by doing your very best each time. You know that you are working hard to complete your personal game in light, not only for humanity, but on behalf of all beings in the universe, just as they do for you. It is your purpose and your pleasure to be part of this experience of life on Earth. There are surprisingly few years remaining on this planet until the end of the human game.

Books by Candace Caddick

In 2009 the Archangels wanted to write a channelled book about the Earth, and help us to see the reality of the world we live on. Planet Earth Today shows a sentient planet of incredible beauty, and a human soul of light. I channelled this book by six Archangels, which was a combination of them explaining and me asking questions. Planet Earth Today is the first book of a trilogy including The Downfall of Atlantis and And I Saw a New Earth that the Archangelic Collective wrote about the coming years, while Guidebook to the Future is designed as a road map leading safely through the coming changes. Stepping Through the Looking Glass introduces the theme of death which we developed in After We Die, and reminds us why ancient Egypt and magic are relevant today. The contents of their books are always relevant to what is happening now, leading into the future.

There is a single story of humanity, a golden book like a long scroll and the three books have been taken from here and typed up. I felt that as long as I was learning new information when writing, information that I couldn't begin to make up, I was on track as an accurate channel. I watched the flow of golden words enter the computer each time until it was the last page of the book. After that my daughter and I checked and checked that I had written it correctly, each paragraph and line examined to see if the golden energy ran through it steadily or if it wavered indicating that it was not quite accurate. Only when we were happy was a section considered complete. Later sometimes I would add more clarity to a section, as my own understanding improved and I could put in more detail. I channel using a combination of sound and sight, and where it is written the best I have been writing down their exact words.

Planet Earth Today

The first book gives background information on the roles of
Earth and the human soul in the universe. Life is experienced so that
they can know themselves and learn why they are alive. Humanity
wished to live on Earth wearing a blindfold; they could see neither
the higher dimensions nor connect to their greater human soul. This
has led to great loneliness and separation as you began to play the
hardest game ever conceived. The Archangel of Darkness presents
his point of view of humanity on Earth, and the Archangels of
Light: Ariel, Esmariel, and Hophriel write with techniques to take
you forward with hope.

This book serves as the introduction to the trilogy as it takes place
before the other two books in time, and the information there about
the planet or Atlantis is not repeated in any other book. However,
each book stands alone and can be read individually.

ISBN 978-0-9565009-0-8

The Downfall of Atlantis

In the story of humanity on Earth, the time spent living and
learning on Atlantis cannot be ignored. During those long years the
darkness gathered around human beings, and science developed a
heartless approach. There were slaves made of combinations of
animals and people and ultimately cloning to keep the wealthy and
important alive indefinitely. Cloning was the final crack in the system
that led to ruin and the end of Atlantis.

Those who refused to go along with the new science escaped at
the end and settled on the surrounding land masses forming the new
post-Atlantean civilisations. The Atlantean influence is explored in

the cultures of Africa, Egypt, Britain and Celtic Europe, as well as North, Central and South America. They learned much from these people in return.

Atlantean civilisation remained intact for a long period of time in Britain because of the ancient sites of power at Avebury, Stonehenge and Glastonbury Tor. When the Shadow in the East pushed westwards into Europe the light of these venerable societies vanished until only the now mythical King Arthur and Merlin were left to protect the Earth from darkness. Their story explains the true significance of the great stone circles, and how we came to forget the real story of Arthur and the sacrifices he made to destroy the invading armies. The connection in a straight line between Atlantis, post-Atlantean civilisations, King Arthur and the Time of Legends is explored so we can remember those things we have forgotten, and not repeat past mistakes.

ISBN 978-0-9565009-1-5

And I Saw A New Earth

Humanity is entering its golden years, when you begin to live as you always intended when you came to Earth. It will be like breathing for the first time, the sweet fresh air that is real life filled with joy, truth and clear-sightedness. And I Saw A New Earth is a channelled book about light, written by those who have ascended in wisdom and understanding and wish to help during a time of rapid change.

During 2012 the Earth received wave after wave of light, enough light to change the way you relate to each other, enough light to show you the lies that have kept you from living in joy. By December the rebirth of Earth herself took place filled with the energy of Spring and fresh beginnings. Humanity can take this energy forward to remove the institutions that failed to work, and restore the balance between work and play. 2012 ended the world you knew: one of

gross inequality and lack of hope. The coming years give you th
chance to build societies of love and fairness, and leave behind th
institutions that failed you in the past. First the energy changes, the
the physical world.

And I Saw a New Earth is written to reassure you that you ca
trust your intuition and your hearts, and that your real future lie
ahead for you to enjoy. Humanity has one of the most importan
roles in the future of the universe.

ISBN: 978-0-9565009-2-2

Guidebook to the Future

There are an overwhelming number of changes taking place ir
the coming years. It's as if you began a long journey without a map
where the road, and even the destination, keeps changing while you
travel. As soon as you become accustomed to one change anothe
one takes its place. It's the beginning of the new 26,000 year galactic
cycle and of the new Earth. Changes are taking place in the higher
dimensions that will affect your society and economies and influence
the forward progress of humanity. Think of this book as a map or
guidebook into the future, showing you the new energy and how it
shapes your individual pathways. We want you to relax, let go and
enjoy the journey.

Angels are beings of love and light, and this book was channelled
to help people look past the radical new changes to the happier
world beyond.

ISBN: 978-0-9565009-3-9

Stepping Through the Looking Glass

This book, the fifth I have written with the Archangels, helps us discover what it is to leave the old world behind and step ahead into the new. We no longer live on the same planet energetically, we are stepping through the looking glass onto a new Earth where we are more aware of the higher dimensions and magic of existence.

The energy on Earth today supports not only change but also finding and making those changes; it does not support the continued patterns of our old ways of living. It's as if a light bulb has come on in a room and we can see clearly, where before a major part of the circuitry of our world was missing. Now the circuit is complete again. The battery has been plugged back in and is filling the world with energy, where we had been running on only the memory of that energy.

This book takes us through the parallels between our time and ancient Egypt, concentrating on the impact the Atlantean survivors made on life there. The Archangels include chapters on magic, to help us break free of out-of-date limitations through understanding and practice. A change has taken place in the way the greater human soul intends to use death. Death can be a tool for consolidation and a splintered soul can become stronger by retiring some souls from the planet while others continue to incarnate.

And finally there is more help on the way as humanity pulls out all the stops to bring through new waves of advanced souls to assist us. It's the beginning of a new future where we mean to succeed and achieve our own ascension.

Writing this book, they would say "more about death, more about magic!" until all the information was included the text.

ISBN: 978-0-9565009-4-6

Books available from online retailers and at:

www.candacecaddick.com

About the Author

I am a teaching Reiki Master who studied for ten years with my Master, prior to initiation in the Usui Shiki Ryoho system of Reiki. Since 1993 I have been practicing my own Reiki daily and my ability to channel has become clearer and stronger, until a few years ago I realised I was able to see the world around me in a way that others did not. My efforts, as I worked with my own Archangelic guides as a channel, were always to unblock and deliver the message clearly, with no preconceptions of what they may say next; to stand well back and just watch and listen.

Before learning Reiki I trained as an economist, worked inside the United States Congress in Washington D.C. as a legislative assistant, and retrained as a nutritional therapist in the UK. Today I lead workshops and tours to the sacred sites in southern England, in addition to teaching Reiki classes and writing books.

If you want to read more from the Archangels and other beings of light, I write a regular channelled blog at:

www.candacecaddick.com

47008390R00094

Printed in Poland
by Amazon Fulfillment
Poland Sp. z o.o., Wrocław